The Smaller Church
in a Super Church Era

The Smaller Church in a Super Church Era

Editors:

Jon Johnston and Bill M. Sullivan

Writers:

Paul M. Bassett, Ron Benefiel, Kenneth Crow,
Charles Gailey, J. Kenneth Grider, John Hawthorne,
B. Edgar Johnson, Jon Johnston, Jack Nash,
Joseph Nielson, Richard Stellway, Bill M. Sullivan

Sponsored by:

The Division of Church Growth,
Church of the Nazarene,
and the
Association of Nazarene Sociologists of Religion (ANSR)

Beacon Hill Press of Kansas City
Kansas City, Missouri

Contents

Foreword

Since the great majority of Churches of the Nazarene are smaller than 100 members, it is appropriate that a book should be written specifically addressed to the pastors and laymen of these churches. I commend Rev. Bill Sullivan, director of the Division of Church Growth, for initiating this project.

The authors have come to grips with very practical considerations relating to the smaller size church. They have dealt with the "pluses" as well as the "minuses," and there are certainly both. The final thrust presents suggested ways in which both the quality and quantity of "body life" may be improved.

Smaller churches are important. It is no disgrace to be small. I have always contended that "super churches" are not primarily determined by size but rather by Spirit. A congregation of any size that gives first priority to the presence and power of the Holy Spirit is "super." Such a church—smaller or larger—like the church at Pentecost, will be vitally concerned with evangelism and church growth. It is no sin to be small. But New Testament churches are not satisfied with smallness and settle for nothing less than growth in the power of the Spirit.

It is my prayer that this book will be used of God to stimulate new life and significant growth in thousands of smaller churches.

—Eugene L. Stowe

Preface

It was a sun-drenched August morning in San Diego. Seated across the breakfast table from me was my friend, Dr. Bill Draper, late president of Point Loma Nazarene College.

In the course of our conversation, I asked this highly respected former pastor just how important he considered the small congregation to be. In this era of "super" everything, does the small church really count?

Without hesitation Bill drew an analogy that warmed my heart. It went something like this:

> You know, Jon, Niagara Falls is a tremendous sight! All of those thousands of tons of wild water gushing over the rocky ledge and free-falling some 150 feet to the maelstrom below. No wonder honeymooners, foreign dignitaries, and about everyone else want to see the awesome sight!

He continued:

> But in spite of its beauty, the fact remains that Canada and the United States would face disaster if they had to depend on this torrent, spectacular though it is, to meet their water needs. Drought would grip the countryside. It is the thousands of small streams throughout the land running softly and quietly—and unnoticed—that channel life-giving water to all areas.

His point was clear. The *Niagara-Falls-type* church, with its touch of the spectacular, captures our attention. And often such attention is deserved. But meanwhile the unobtrusive *small-stream-type* of congregation often goes unnoticed, or if noticed, it is minimized. Therefore its minister and members are lost in the shuffle.

Unfortunately, many overlook the fact that the small church is the virtual "lifeblood" of the Kingdom. Instead of its suffering feelings of frustration and discouragement, it should be filled with assurance and thanksgiving.

A few months after the breakfast with Dr. Draper, another Bill—Rev. Bill Sullivan—asked me to bring together the sociologists of the Church to find ways in which their expertise could be channelled into the outreach program of the denomination. As a result the Association of Nazarene Sociologists of Religion (ANSR) was founded in January of 1982.

At that initial meeting the group's attention gravitated toward the subject of the small congregation—one with a membership of 100 or less.

We deeply empathized with its problems but also rejoiced over its unique opportunities. We did *not* consider small to be synonymous with superior, or even satisfactory, nongrowth to be virtuous, nor superchurches to be devoid of worth.

In the course of our meeting Rev. Sullivan challenged us to write our thoughts and inspirations on paper, and this book was conceived. Each of the sociologists present agreed to write a chapter: Rev. Ron Benefiel (pastor of Los Angeles First Church of the Nazarene); Professor Kenneth Crow (Mid-America Nazarene College, Olathe, Kans.); Dr. Charles Gailey (Nazarene Theological Seminary, Kansas City); Dr. Joseph Nielson (Olivet Nazarene College, Kankakee, Ill.); Dr. Richard Stellway (Northwest Nazarene College, Nampa, Ida.); and Dr. Jon Johnston (Pepperdine University, Malibu, Calif.).

Then, the following guest writers were asked to join in the assignment: Drs. Paul Bassett and J. Kenneth Grider (professors at Nazarene Theological Seminary); Dr. B. Edgar Johnson (general secretary of the Church of the Nazarene); Rev. Jack Nash (pastor of Northridge, Calif., Community Church of the Nazarene); and Rev. Bill Sullivan (director of the Division of Church Growth, Church of the Nazarene). Later, Prof. John Hawthorne from Olivet Nazarene College joined Dr. Nielson in the work on his chapter.

Two persons provided invaluable assistance to the project. Rev. Dale Jones, statistical analyst in the Church Growth division at Headquarters, coordinated the publication process. And Dr. Fred Parker, retired book editor of the Nazarene Publishing House, did the final editing.

Ours has been a labor of love—but a labor nevertheless. We set high standards for ourselves and had to conform to the constraints of a tight schedule, the latter in order to release our work on the occasion of the 75th Anniversary Celebration of the Church of the Nazarene.

It has been our purpose to analyze the characteristics of the small congregation and to offer some constructive guidelines for maximizing its potential in the Kingdom.

And it is our hope that you, the reader, will gain a clearer perspective of (and a deeper appreciation for) those *thousands of small streams that run softly, quietly, and unnoticed* throughout the countryside—bringing spiritual sustenance and nourishment to a thirsty land.

JON JOHNSTON

David in Goliath's World

by Dr. Jon Johnston

Our Colossus Complex

Have you noticed that it's usually the little persons who get put down or kicked around? Some call it "size discrimination"; others refer to it as the "colossus complex."

Take sports. Except for horse racing jockeys and midget wrestlers, small athletes hardly survive—much less star. In novels, it's invariably the lanky cowboy or the tall-and-handsome suitor who commands the affections of the beautiful heroine.

Researcher Ralph Keyes concludes that the mere possession of a towering physique means money in the bank. Statuesque people receive higher salaries, occupy more important positions, and wield greater influence.[1] Put another way, they have less of a necessity to marry the boss's daughter (or son).

DR. JON JOHNSTON
teaches sociology at Pepperdine University, Malibu, Calif. He has taught at Mount Vernon Nazarene College, Mount Vernon, Ohio, and is an ordained elder in the Church of the Nazarene.
He serves as chairman of the Association of Nazarene Sociologists of Religion. Dr. Johnston has written for several publications, and has authored *Will Evangelicalism Survive Its Own Popularity?*

When it comes to people, mere size counts. The conscious or unconscious awareness of this fact prompts many to resort to wearing elevator shoes and most of us to purposely exaggerate our height. Basketball programs have become a joke. Even the shortest guy on the team is rarely listed as less than six feet.

One more thing. We typically overestimate the stature of those we most respect. If you doubt this, glance at a crayon picture of people sketched by a kindergarten pupil. Dad, Mom, teacher, and best buddies are given gigantic proportions.

The colossus complex has become an enormous part of our national psyche. As with people, so with other areas of our cultural existence. Kirkpatrick Sale, in his book titled *Human Scale*, lists some indications of our preoccupation with bigness:

> In the U.S. there are eleven different sizes of olives. The smallest size is "jumbo." [Similarly, locating a menu with a "small" pizza is about as easy as finding blue M and M's.]
>
> The U.S. manufactures the largest newspapers in the world. The *New York Times*, the largest of them all, for an average Sunday in November, *any* November, weighs about ten pounds. It takes 840 acres of Canadian trees to produce one average Sunday's edition, more than enough wood to build 100 three-bedroom ranch houses. It also costs ten cents a copy in New York City Sanitation Department expenses just to pick up the littered copies on Monday morning.
>
> American advertising expresses its most important messages in superlatives about size: the biggest shopping centers . . . the nation's largest airlines with the world's biggest fleet of widebodies . . . Big Macs, Whoppers, Jumbo Cokes, Green Giant . . . king size, extralarge.[2]

Unfortunately, we also realize that such grand-scale tastes necessitate ever-increasing incomes. Big costs more—

always—even though the man behind the ice-cream counter tells us that we're saving money by ordering three scoops.

It all comes down to a conclusion reached by anthropologist Edward C. Stewart. We Americans cannot resist the overpowering temptation to quantify. Like the Pythagoreans of ancient Greece, we believe that the essence of quality is measurement—and that success is gauged by statistics. When our numbers and dimensions grow we're pleased; when they decrease we panic.

What a far cry from a society like the Kpelle of Liberia, who never count their chickens for fear that some harm will come to them.[3]

But the crucial question is: Does our compulsion for bigness stop at the front door of the church? Or have we allowed it to become our primary reason for existence—our predominant measure of success? Put another way, have we allowed this secular fiction that bigger is always better to cripple us with feelings of worthless inferiority when we fail to measure up statistically?

Filed Under "Miscellaneous"

The majority of the congregations of all denominations are small. Nevertheless, ecclesiastical opinion is strongly biased in the direction of largeness. Big edifices. Armies of associate ministers. "Dare to top that" programming. Membership rolls and attendance figures that stagger the imagination—enticing church growth analysts to attempt to encapsulate a "bigness" formula.

Meanwhile, the small congregation is considered almost an embarrassment to the Kingdom. Hokey. Out of step. Like a cold sore on the lip of life. Or, to use an expression that Fritz Ridenour uses in another context, "with about as much influence as a boxkite on a radar screen."

But, the little church isn't ignored completely. It is continually reminded that it, too, can someday become a big church—with harder work, more devotion to the task, and more attention to the "guaranteed" formulas for big growth. There are exceptions but, as a rule, the small congregation is often encouraged to adopt the large church model. It is goaded into the prospect that some day it, too, may be in a position to boast about its size.

The unfortunate truth is that, all too often, people arrive at unfair conclusions about the little church that remains little. These range from assuming a severe lack of dedication to making insinuations about a lack of know-how. A kind of dinosaur-age mentality.

And how about the pastor of the pint-size congregation? Many perceive him as either "on his way up" or "on his way out." They think that any preacher worth his salt won't allow himself to be relegated to a small church for very long. As if smaller churches were merely stepping-stones to bigger churches—the "minor leagues" of ecclesiastical structure.

Feeling the pressure from such inaccurate concepts, some ministers grope for relief. Many settle for the mere illusion of bigness without the foundation of solid growth. This may bolster a severely deflated self-image—and even help quiet criticism—but it is artificial and often counterproductive.

Playing Make-believe

The most frequently employed method for providing the illusion of bigness is the familiar rally day. Well-conceived rally days can result in great dividends for God's kingdom. Momentum and morale increase; new prospects are introduced to the church. And for a short duration, they provide the two valued commodities that the typical big church offers on a regular basis: celebration and entertainment.

Nevertheless, the underlying goal of rally day is too often *numbers for numbers' sake*. And if the goals are reached, the numbers are waved like a trophy for all to see.

I have to chuckle when I recall a rally day incident of my childhood. It was district contest time, and the pastor in a town nearby was pitted against a much larger city church. He fumed a lot, especially when they ribbed him about his chances. Added to his distress was the fact that the prize offered to the pastor of the winning church was an all-expense-paid vacation to a highly desirable resort.

The contest lasted 12 weeks, as I recall, and after 10 our friend's church was, as expected, considerably behind, despite his valiant efforts. Hating the whole idea of contests, bigness, and all the negative attitudes that it engendered, the pastor even hesitated to ask God for a miracle. God probably didn't think that he needed or deserved a resort vacation anyway.

But still feeling goaded by fellow competitors, and wanting to make a point, this minister decided to take things in his own hands. He devised an all-out effort for the final day and announced his plan on the next to the last Sunday. He had arranged for a TV celebrity well-known to children throughout southern California to make an appearance on the final Sunday.

The plan was for "Space Cadet" to land his helicopter on a nearby vacant lot and to share a few words with the throngs who would gather—many of whom were parents dragged there by their enthusiastic children. Church ushers would be stationed on the premises, ready to count every human being in the vicinity.

This preacher needed numbers. Big numbers. And guess what—he got them. He not only won the contest, he thoroughly buried his flabbergasted competition. And to the beautiful resort he flew. Justice had been "satisfied." Such desperate attempts to achieve size recognition, however, have little value in the long run.

In his "Foreword" of Robert E. Maner's book, titled *Making the Small Church Grow,* William M. Greathouse speaks of the very real possibility of becoming a "beleagured and bewildered small-church pastor."[4]

Afflicted by such a condition, it is easy for him to develop defeating and illusionary tactics. The result is an acute sensitivity that causes defensive aggressiveness and unreal guilt that maximizes stress. His blurred vision produces an unclear sense of mission. Furthermore, the pastor who possesses any of the above reactions tends to pass them on to his vulnerable laity.

Out of the Soup!

With all of this in mind, how can the pastor of the small church and his laity

- gain a sense of *authentic purpose*—without developing false pride;
- diligently work within the context of their *growth potential*—without becoming a slave to numbers;
- fully appreciate their opportunity for a *unique ministry*—without resenting their "big brothers"?

Regardless of those voices that echo the "bigger is better" theme, it is imperative that the leader and constituency of the small congregation *not* lose heart. The temptation to despair must give way to a renewed spirit—a rekindled sense of purpose and mission.

The small church must begin developing the right perspective. Facts and situations may look completely different when viewed through an energizing frame of reference. Few could argue with these goals. But the crucial question is "How?" Consider the following.

1. *God's Scorecard*

Our Heavenly Father is very concerned about persons as persons. Of course, this is not to say that He does not care about large social bodies, such as nations. His tender loving care for Israel is enough to dispel such a notion.

Nevertheless, our Divine Master has always focused on individuals within the masses. I paraphrase the words of Reuben Welch: God sees and loves *you* as *you* are, where *you* are, right now.[5]

Since we experience tailor-made concern and attention from the Creator of the universe, it seems to matter little to Him whether we assemble in a small, a middle-sized, or a gigantic congregation.

No wonder His Son, and our Savior, spent so much time ministering to individuals. The adulterous woman at Jacob's Well. The demon-possessed recluse in the Gerasene graveyard.

Like His Father, Christ's primary concern was for individuals. The health of their bodies. The quality of their hearts. And it seems only fair to declare that He most often expressed that concern in small groupings—the eyeball-to-eyeball kind. Where such things as smiles, nervous twitches, and wrinkled foreheads are readily detected. Where confrontation is authentic. This can happen in a large social body, but more frequently it occurs in a small group.

There were the accusation-hurling sessions with the Pharisees. The intimate, heart-changing discussions with *His congregation of a dozen.* With the "inner three" on the Mount of Transfiguration. At the Last Supper.

And to those same disciples He declared that wherever and whenever twos and threes are gathered together in His name, He is there. Actually present. So He can be felt and worshiped.

Granted, our Lord fed the hungry bodies and souls of pushing, demanding crowds—like the 5,000 on the hillside overlooking the Sea of Galilee. But even there He gave great attention to individuals. And most of the time, He ministered to individuals in small groups.

How can we dare minimize the importance of that which He and His Father considered so basic? So essential? So crucial?

2. *Not All That Shabby*

In the process of constructing a helpful perspective, a second thought must be fully grasped. *A small congregation has definite structural and functional advantages over a large one.* In a similar way, anthropologists are quick to point out that a clan is superior to an entire tribe in meeting certain vital needs of a preliterate society.[6]

Although a later chapter focuses on these specific advantages, allow me to illustrate the point.

My cousin, Don Golliher, enjoys recalling memories of his childhood days in a small congregation. That congregation was the only Church of the Nazarene in the coal mining community of Murphysboro, Ill. And it was small. In a recent article he spoke appreciatingly of the cultural education he received in this humble setting.[7]

But it is another of his descriptions that makes an indelible impression on my mind. This one centers on what he concluded to be his congregation's special penchant for continually monitoring the spiritual condition of each person attending. According to Don, definite signals were released and intercepted in the course of a typical church service.

For example, the congregation was asked to kneel and pray. And, sure enough, the person who had fallen from grace, or at least was slipping, remained upright—sitting there like a "great speckled bird" for all soul-surveyors to behold. Not incidentally, the pastor always had the best visual vantage point to do such monitoring as he knelt beside his pulpit and faced his flock.

A "popcorn" testimony session was included in most services. Once again, the members' devotion was gauged. And the one who remained unresponsive (during the long pause after everyone else had spoken) was suspected of being discouraged, burdened, or on the threshold of backsliding.

On occasion, the pastor received positive signals from someone he had reason to believe was having difficulty. The mettle of the suspected one could be tested by calling on that person to lead in group prayer or join others in raising a hand during a song.

The point is this. In a small congregation, like the one described above, there exists the opportunity to lovingly force a readout on everyone's up-to-date spiritual condition. It might be called "accountability."

As a result, individuals are not hidden among the crowd. And the difficulty exposed by such monitoring allows the close-knit fellowship to join in the rescue. At its best the small church is a kind of *rescue squad*—prepared for emergencies. Carl S. Dudley, in his book titled *Making the Small Church Effective,* aptly describes this rescue-oriented environment:

> In a big world, the small church has remained INTIMATE.
> In a fast world, the small church has been STEADY.
> In an expensive world, the small church has remained PLAIN.
> In a complex world, the small church has remained SIMPLE.
> In a rational world, the small church has kept FEELING.
> In a mobile world, the small church has been an ANCHOR.
> In an anonymous world, the small church CALLS US BY NAME.[8]

Admittedly, the larger congregation has *its own* list of advantages: specialized ministries, a larger work force, more people with multiple talents, more economic resources, and ministers who have the luxury of being able to delegate—freeing up more time for sermon preparation.

All of this implies that the "which is best" question is futile. Small *and* large congregations are *both* better and worse than each other. It all depends on the specific goals in mind. Nevertheless, the point can be emphatically made: small and large churches alike should begin recognizing the unique assets of the other. In addition, they must consider one another to be of equal value in God's diversified kingdom. Full realization of this fact will result in a warm spirit of mutual respect and genuine teamwork—the kind that befits His redeemed community of believers.

3. *Pew Packers Anonymous*

A final consideration is especially worthy of careful attention, for it gets to the root of our basic motivation.

The primary task of the church, be it small or large, is NOT merely to produce people to fill empty pews. Rather, it is to offer everyone the love of God in the name of Jesus.

That ministry can be accomplished only when *His* presence is the focal point of attention. When it is seen that it is *He* who is the force for miracles that occur when His disciples are assembled. And to the degree that those disciples are infused with *His* presence, they are able to effectively minister in preaching, teaching, benevolence, and fellowship.

Author Paul Madsen aptly puts it:

> Simply to seek for people is selfish. To seek for people that their lives be enriched and changed is a totally different purpose. Pews can be full, but churches can still be sterile and empty of significance if there is no vision of mission and commitment to that mission.[9]

22

Seeking numbers for numbers' sake is a form of idolatry. But to desire that individuals will assemble for the purpose of drawing vitality from God is commendable. In fact it alone prepares the church to fulfill its mission in the world. The acceptance of this basic principle gives the knotty and much-debated question of "seeking numbers" a new perspective.

The question is not: Shall we reach out for people? The Great Commission (Matt. 28:19-20) puts that inquiry to rest. It is clear enough that we must use all means to draw those with a "God-shaped void" in their lives.

To commit ourselves to the goal of remaining small is no answer. Smug, ingrown, exclusive "holy clubs" bring discredit to the Kingdom. Smallness, like bigness, is an idolatrous shrine that far too many bow before. Again, God is not the private possession of either the large mass or the small enclave. He belongs to individuals.

In short, the attempt to grow is consistent with the biblical imperative—but for the specific reason of facilitating the God-man connection. As many as possible must be warmly welcomed into the koinonia—the worshiping fellowship of the family of God.[10] But we are not merely to count their heads, test church growth theories, produce a more conspicuous "splash," or advance a preacher's personal aspirations. Rather, *each* new person is to be seen as an infinitely precious individual in God's sight. Not a means to some end. An end. Period.

And as simple as it may sound, the dominant desire of our hearts must be to hear *each* individual confidently sing—with a heartfelt testimony that rings: "Jesus loves *me*, this *I* know. For the Bible tells *me* so!"

Personal Recollections

My own childhood was embellished by the influence of eight small congregations in five states. In case you haven't guessed, my dad was a pastor.

There was never a time that I felt deprived, cramped, or embarrassed about being closely identified with a small group of God's people. Perhaps I was too tone-deaf to the secular value system. Or maybe, back then, even that system didn't make such a big deal over numbers.

Oh, there were needs, all right. Plenty of them. Dad's first church, constructed in the middle of the Depression, was completed only because of his God-given ability to solicit materials from businessmen. The teen groups were always small—and the girls never seemed to be much to look at. As for the special music for the services, well, it's fair to say that it operated under the principle that participation is better than perfection.

And for some strange reason, it seemed like every church building had a horrendous leak in the roof—invariably in the worst possible place. One such visitation from nature pretty much wiped out my dad's treasured books in his study.

But in spite of such "minor" inconveniences, I learned a great deal. I mean about life. Like feeling the shock waves when someone let down, or even quit. Like witnessing the survival tactics of my father, when his pastoral vote was uncomfortably close or his meager salary made living unusually tight. Like experiencing the "goldfish-bowl existence" of being a preacher's kid.

I stand in humble gratitude for this heritage. And I write about the small church with a sense of deep conviction and appreciation.

Today while acknowledging the fact that many big churches have much to say in their favor, I choose to identify with a small congregation. Where everyone is called upon to shoulder the load, and where caring is intimate and inclusive. And where individuals, represented by statistics, take an overwhelming precedence over the statistics themselves.

It is churches like those of my childhood and the one to

which I presently belong that predominate in our land. And they are its salt (Matt. 5:13) and light (Matt. 6:14). Like cities on hills (Matt. 5:14-16) and miniature "colonies of heaven."

In a society that is plagued with an acute condition of "colossus complex," such congregations may seem unimpressive. In reality their impact is far-reaching and their reward is eternal.

DISCUSSION QUESTIONS

1. Would you prefer to be taller? Why?
2. What kinds of snap conclusions do people reach about little churches that remain little? Which of these are justified?
3. Why did Jesus spend so much time in small gatherings?
4. Do you agree with Paul Madsen's statement: "Simply to seek people is selfish"? Why?
5. What is your reaction to the "Space Cadet" incident?
6. Reflect on your experience with, and opinion of, small congregations. Cite positives and negatives.

Are Small Churches Really Beautiful?

by Dr. Charles Gailey

The building was really just a converted house with abandoned theater seats for chairs. But it housed a small congregation of great spiritual fervor. There was an aura of glory about the place, and the people really cared and loved. That church changed my life!

After a decade of attention being given to large congregations, there is a resurgence of interest in the small church. A number of books have been published extolling the virtues of small congregations. Perhaps the best known is *Small Churches Are Beautiful.*[1] In this chapter we will consider these questions: Are small congregations *really* beautiful? Should small churches have negative feelings about themselves?

DR. CHARLES R. GAILEY
teaches anthropology and missions at Nazarene Theological Seminary, Kansas City. He taught at Eastern Nazarene College, part of the time chairing the Department of Sociology. He served as a missionary to Swaziland and received a commendation from that nation's prime minister. Dr. Gailey belongs to the American Sociological Association and is listed in the *International Scholars Directory* and the *Centre d'Analyse et de Recherche Documentaires pour L'Afrique Noire.*

What are the unique strengths and weaknesses of the small congregation?

You Are Not Alone

Is your congregation a small one? Join the club! Most congregations are. In fact, throughout history, and in various denominations and countries of the world, the majority of congregations have had fewer than 100 members. Recently, perhaps because we have entered the "superchurch" era, the small congregation has been derided as inferior. The stereotype of a small church is one that is backward, boring, and somehow a failure. This may not be so at all.

Actually, there are several reasons why a congregation may be small: First, as the Body of Christ multiplies (and multiply it should), it will spawn congregations that will usually be small at the outset. These congregations are now small, but are expected to grow.

Second, some churches are small because they are in rural locations or villages where a static or declining population may provide a restricted population base on which to draw.

Third, there are small congregations that exist in cities. For some reason these congregations have not grown, though they should.

Fourth, a congregation may elect to send members from their church to start other churches and as a result limit the size of their own congregation.

Most congregations of various denominations are small. For example, 55 percent of the churches of the Church of the Nazarene have fewer than 75 members. Fifty-seven percent of United Methodist churches have an average attendance of less than 75 at the main service.[2]

If your church is small because it is new or because it is located in an area of declining population or is in a rural area,

27

there is no reason for you to be negative about it. Your church is not alone! And being small is not all bad. There are real strengths, as well as weaknesses, in the smaller congregation.

The size of a congregation can be a plus as well as a minus. Too often in the past smallness has been seen only as a weakness, and in recent books smallness has perhaps been overglorified. *What is needed is a balanced view.*

By presenting this balanced view we do not mean to imply that one is superior to the other. Both larger and smaller congregations have advantages and disadvantages. Both have their unique roles to play in the Body of Christ.

Fellowship and Warm Fuzzies

Perhaps the biggest plus of the smaller congregation is the warmth of its group fellowship. Everyone knows everyone else—and truly cares. This is the important biblical concept of koinonia.

The smaller church lends itself easily to what Charles Horton Cooley called "face-to-face interaction with others."[3] The sense of supportive fellowship and community can be very great in this type of group. The smaller congregation, dominated by love, can form warm primary groups. Such groupings are desperately needed in the contemporary world that is so often characterized by fractured relationships. Töennies called this "community" as opposed to "society."[4] In contemporary language, "warm fuzzies"! It's difficult not to be noticed in a small congregation!

> Linda was a talented, dynamic teenager who went away to college in a Western state. She was an award-winning athlete, an accomplished musician, and an experienced youth worker. Linda, the "star of the show" in her local church, felt "lost" and alone in the big church she now attended. She filled out a card saying that she was interested in

helping in several programs of the church, but no one ever called her. Linda then turned to a smaller congregation.

Moberg has pointed out that when congregations grow larger, there is a tendency to shift much of the work of the church to paid workers. This tends to eat away at the close ties of the congregation. He states: "The spontaneity, informality and intimacy of primary group interaction tend to disappear; laymen are used proportionately less."[5]

Members of large churches have also been found in some studies to shoulder less responsibility and give less because they tend to assume "someone else is taking care of it." The degree of participation[6] of the individual church member shows an inverse correlation with the size of the church. Oates puts it this way: "The participation of the individual church members has decreased in proportion to the increase in the size of the congregation."[7] As the church grows, it seems that the average member's sense of responsibility to give, work, and participate decreases. There is an increasing tendency to "let George (or Mary or John) do it."

Several authors have noted that there is usually a higher percentage of members present in the small congregation than the large one in a given worship service.[8] The reason is easy to see: in the smaller congregation one is more likely to be missed! Members of large churches tend to count the empty pews; in the small congregation they count faces.

These weaknesses, of course, do not have to exist in the large church. One solution is to build more "small group" fellowship into the larger body. Wise pastors of large congregations have done this by forming "circles of concern." The smaller congregation should, however, be encouraged to know that the "primary group" characteristic of their congregation is an extremely precious commodity.

We should be aware that the "strength" of close fellowship in the small church may also become a weakness. It is possible for the smaller congregation to become exclusive and ingrown. Petty jealousies and bickering may then break out. Backbiting may contaminate the small church that lacks vision for outreach and obedience to Christ. Usually, however, even where there are interpersonal difficulties, there is an underlying concern for others in the smaller congregation.

Even if there is no internal dissension, a cozy attitude of intimate friendship may be allowed to actually repel visitors. Strangers may be looked upon as intruders.

> *The day after Ken and I were married was a Sunday, and we looked for the nearest church. It was a rural area. Our attendance at church that morning created a sensation.*
>
> *As we walked into the church every head seemed to swivel in our direction. Admittedly, we were "city slickers" and we did have nice clothes, but when the eyes of many remained fixed on us throughout the service, it was too much! I never will forget the pianist. She didn't look at the keyboard, the music, or the songleader—she had eyes only for us! How she could keep playing the hymns while staring constantly our way was a wonder! The whole congregation seemed to shout—"Where did these creatures come from?"*

An "us" and "they" attitude may develop in the small congregation, which can insure that the small congregation stays that way permanently.

Every small church needs to determine to follow Jesus very closely and to always be obedient in carrying out a responsible mission for Him. Such a congregation will not be entrapped by its potential weaknesses, but will instead come to realize their God-given potential.

Crisis Support

Crisis support is a close corollary to primary group friendships. When someone is in trouble in the small congregation, everybody knows it.

> *When baby Laura was sick in the night, church members began calling me the next morning. Someone had seen our*

lights on at 2 a.m. After the calls, several meals and pies for
dessert were sent in. We really felt the support of the church
during this time.

Every member of the smaller congregation is part of the
potential support group in a crisis. The personal touch is very
evident. Each individual is extremely important to the group.
The congregation more readily accepts individual differences. There is a place for everyone to be loved and respected.[9]

When death occurs, the entire congregation journeys
through "the valley of the shadow" with the bereaved. Often,
the whole church turns out for the funeral. By contrast, a
member of a large congregation may not even know the deceased.

The relational strength of the smaller congregation can
also be lost. Negative attitudes can displace supportive ones.
When Christ is not followed closely, people may begin to say,
"Well, we've done all that we can do," or tragically, "We'll
never get *that* family into the church." And perhaps even
worse, "I'll never help her. I remember what *she* did to *me*."
Such attitudes kill the essential character of the church.

Every small congregation should relish the unique opportunities that they have for supportive acts and attitudes.
And they should be constantly on guard against negative
viewpoints and decisions.

Human Development

Small congregations have produced some of the great
leaders of the church. It should not surprise us that this is so,
for the small church provides great opportunity for development of the potential of each individual. I know of one
New England congregation with an average attendance of
about 25 that has produced three full-time pastors in the past
five years.

There are basic reasons why the harvest of leadership should be great in small churches. One is that smallness usually demands a higher percentage of participation, and often at an earlier age.

> Joe's children marvel that he was elected Sunday School superintendent at the wise old age of 16. In the large church they attend it would be unthinkable to give a teenager such responsibility.

Secondly, the smaller church often provides a congenial setting in which individual talents can be exercised and proven.

A good small congregation is an effective seedbed of leadership. On the other hand, the program of a smaller church is necessarily limited. There will not be enough people to divide up into a number of "special interest" groups. Arthur Tennies has pointed out how this "lack of critical mass" can affect churches. A "world hunger" group, for example, may draw only four people in the small church, but 24 may attend such a group in a large church. In both cases seven percent of the membership have responded. But in the small church, the four people who have come feel that "not enough people are interested," and drop the group. In contrast, the group of 24 develops into an enthusiastic organization. In one church the same small percentage "produced a critical mass—twenty-four people—and in the other it did not."[10]

The smaller congregation should be recognized as an effective means of human development, but it is limited in the extent of its programming.

Knowledgeable Shepherds

When the "flock" is small, the shepherd can know all of his sheep in an in-depth relationship. The backgrounds, the life-styles, and even the hangups of members of a small congregation will register with the pastor. By contrast, the pastoral staff of a large church is unlikely to have such intimate contact.

Such a situation may contribute to greater efficiency in meeting the members' needs and fulfilling the pastoral task.

When Mrs. Crowthers gets upset, I can see it by the look in her eyes.

This strength is at least partially offset by the financial fact that the pastor of a small congregation "costs more" on a per capita basis. In other words, a smaller number of people are contributing to the pastor's salary. The "in-depth" care of the pastor of a small congregation will probably demand a bigger percentage of the annual budget.

Flexibility

It is easy for a smaller congregation to be flexible in structure and program. Opportunities can be grasped, changes can be made, and new ideas can be introduced very quickly. Why is this so? Because a smaller number of people are the "decision-makers" in the congregation. A ponderous bureaucracy of boards and subcommittees is not needed in the smaller congregation. This "plus," however, can also become a liability if the "decision-makers" of the congregation settle for low expectations. They may turn their great advantage into shame with *rut* resistance to *change!* If they are content with spur-of-the-moment programs without structure ("Who would like to lead the singing tonight?"), the church will suffer. But if the leaders of the church will accept the challenge, great flexibility and forward-looking programs will result.

Community Posture

Smaller congregations are often located in smaller communities. In this setting the pastor is often looked upon as a community leader. The clergy is one of the key professional categories in town, along with the doctors, lawyers, and teachers. As a result, the pastor of the small church often has a community posture and influence that is out of proportion to the size of the congregation.

> Over at Jefferson, Pastor Smith was elected chaplain of the Fire Department. For the last eight years he has built a solid image of ministry in the town. As he puts it, "The community leaders know who I am and where our church is."
>
> He often gets called over his C-B by his handle of "Padre." When the community of Jefferson needs help, it's "Padre, have you got your ears on?"

The "other side of the coin" in this case is the fact that the smaller congregation usually has a narrow financial base from which to operate. The minister may have an important community profile, but the funds available to capitalize on that profile may be very limited. This is a great challenge to the smaller congregation.

Uniquely Suited

In this chapter we have suggested some strengths and weaknesses of the smaller congregation. The balance sheet is by no means lopsided! The small church *does* have a special ministry to fulfill that has been historically and sociologically validated. As Christensen has put it: "Small congregations are uniquely suited to helping persons discover the reconciling love of God and their own growth as Christians in a complete, life style-oriented way not usually attained in larger congregations."[11]

Family-style fellowship, crisis support, pastoral shepherding, participation and the development of the individual may be handled just as well (and, in some cases, more so) in the small congregation as in the large.

The real question, then, is not one of size, but of *obedience*. Obedience to God, to His Word, and to His will is the only action that makes a congregation really *beautiful*.

DISCUSSION QUESTIONS

1. Would you prefer to be a member of a small or a large congregation? Why?
2. What are the real advantages of a "primary group"?
3. In what ways do the "dangers" of being small outweigh the disadvantages?
4. How can koinonia be more effectively developed in a smaller congregation? (See definitions of this word in chapter 1, footnote 10.)
5. When you think of a really "beautiful" congregation, what comes to mind?
6. What are some effective ways you can turn *your* church's weaknesses into strengths? On an individual level? On a group level?

3

Little Is Much—With God

by Dr. J. Kenneth Grider

The Bible is replete with examples of how God accomplished His purposes with a limited number of people. The classic illustration of this is the story of Gideon. A powerful enemy host was put to flight by him and his small band of 300 dedicated soldiers.

The 32,000 men originally drafted were too many. They probably could have subdued Midian, but this would not have proved that it was because God had helped them. So in the first screening "twenty-two thousand men left" (Judg. 7:3). But God said the remaining 10,000 were still too many. For the further necessary cutback these were taken to the water, where by a unique test God sifted out the small group that He wanted. God told Gideon, "Separate those who lap the water with their tongues like a dog from those who kneel

DR. J. KENNETH GRIDER
is professor of theology at Nazarene Theological Seminary, Kansas City, where he has served since 1953. Previously, this teacher, writer, and preacher taught at Hurlet Nazarene College, Glasgow, and Pasadena College (now Point Loma Nazarene College), Pasadena, Calif. Dr. Grider has written for *Christianity Today* and *Christian Century*, and is listed in *Who's Who in American Education*.

down to drink" (Judg. 7:5). Only 300 men lapped the water, and God said, "With the three hundred men that lapped I will save you and give the Midianites into your hands" (Judg. 7:7). And that is just what God did—and so He works today.

1. *With respect to the small congregation, we need to keep in mind the truth expressed by the songwriter, "Little is much when God is in it."*

The small groups of people often mentioned in Scripture show that "small" is significant when God is on their side. For example, when things looked bad for Judah, with Sennacherib of Assyria being so belligerent, Isaiah sent King Hezekiah this encouraging message from God: "Out of Jerusalem will come a remnant, and out of Mount Zion a band of survivors" (2 Kings 19:31). Again when Judah rebelled against God in the late eighth century B.C., Isaiah realized that there was a "remnant" (KJV) who did not lift their puny fists against Ultimatus. He took courage and said, "Unless the Lord Almighty had left us some survivors, we would have become like Sodom, we would have been like Gomorrah" (Isa. 1:9).

Moses' rod, a widow's small amount of flour and oil, a still small voice, Gideon's small army, the faithful of Israel—were all "much" when God was figured in.

Likewise, the early churches mentioned in the New Testament, though probably rather small, were truly significant. We conclude that they were small partly because they usually met in the homes of believers—and also because they were not allowed to own property. Referring to Priscilla and Aquila, his "fellow workers in Christ Jesus," Paul says, "Greet also the church that meets at their house" (Rom. 16:5). In opening his brief letter to his "dear friend" Philemon, he greets him and "the church that meets in your home" (v. 2). And in the closing of the Colossian letter, Paul says, "Give my greetings to the brothers at Laodicea, and to Nympha and the church in her house" (4:15).

From jail to jail, from martyrdom to martyrdom, the apostles preached Christ. We read, "Day after day, in the temple courts and from house to house, they never stopped teaching and proclaiming the good news that Jesus is the Christ" (Acts 5:42). And, in what seems to be a reference to receiving the Lord's Supper in their houses we read, "They broke bread in their homes and ate together with glad and sincere hearts, praising God and enjoying the favor of all the people" (Acts 2:46-47).

Even after the learned Apollos, with his "thorough knowledge of the Scriptures" (Acts 18:24), had spoken at Ephesus "with great fervor and taught about Jesus accurately" (v. 25), the church that was present was composed of only "twelve men in all" (Acts 19:7) as Paul visited it.

Scripture never states that any of the churches were either large or small, although it sometimes states that "many" people in a given place believed the gospel. In the 112 instances where the word *church* is found in the New Testament, the size of the churches does not seem to be of great significance to the writers. We read of "the whole church" (Acts 15:22), of churches "everywhere" (1 Cor. 4:17), of "a great persecution [that] broke out against the church" (Acts 8:1), of fear coming upon "the whole church" (Acts 5:11), and that they "added to their number daily those who were being saved" (Acts 2:47). But though the New Testament writers were not much interested in the specific numbers of believers in the various churches, the present-day churches are very concerned. Back then they did not seem to have had what they thought of as big churches and small ones. *The church was the church, and that was that—and it was composed of those who believed savingly that God had raised from the dead the Christ who had been crucified.*

While church size *per se* was not a primary interest of Scripture, the *quality* of the Christians in the churches and their evangelistic fervor through which the churches would grow was indeed of primary importance. The apostle Paul's letters written to these various churches reveal this fact. The New Testament churches were probably not very large, but at such places as Thessalonica and Philippi and Ephesus, there were significant groups of early Christian believers.

The church at Philippi set a special example in financial support of the ministry (Phil. 4:15-16); the group at Berea specialized in the study of Scripture (Acts 17:11), and the Thessalonians were strong on witnessing and evangelism (1 Thess. 1:7-9). Although the church at Corinth was problem-filled, it was still a prominent congregation, partly because it was the inspiration for Paul's instruction on how to deal with problems in local churches! The church at Rome, so small that it seems to have met at the "house" of "Priscilla and Aquila" (Rom. 16:3, 5), occasioned Paul's extended and most theological epistle.

And in the intervening centuries, such churches and groups have often been strategic. The church at Lugdunum (the modern Lyons) in what is now France was not large, meeting underground as it needed to do in the late second century under the leadership of Irenaeus. But it gave that missionary bishop a place of ministry and permitted him to write voluminously and significantly—especially against the Gnostics. These heretics were trying hard to win Christians over to a dualistic view that denied Christ's full humanity and to deprecate the world that God had created.

In the late fourth and early fifth centuries, the church at Hippo in North Africa was in a nowhere town and not exceedingly large. Yet it was the focus of Augustine's ministry and to some extent formed the background for his significant theological writings.

The church at Wittenberg, in Saxony, was not exceptionally large, but it, too, was strategic. Its pastor, Martin Luther, also a professor in the town's recently founded university, posted on its door in Latin, for debate among the scholars, 95 points, mainly about true repentance. The outcome was that the whole Western Church was soon convulsed (and purified) by a reforming of Christian faith according to the New Testament pattern.

A small congregation was significant at a little meeting place on Aldersgate Street in London where John Wesley received his strangely warmed heart on May 24, 1738. The person leading that small gathering was not well educated and was required simply to read to the group instead of preaching a sermon of his own making. He read to the group from Martin Luther's preface to the Epistle to the Romans. And John Wesley, who had been searching so diligently for the evangelical faith that Peter Böhler and other Moravians enjoyed, came to the end of his quest. That afternoon he had attended a service in the huge St. Paul's Cathedral, but it was at a small gathering of believers that night that he had his memorable conversion experience.

2. *Another important biblical basis for the significance of a small church congregation is the nature of the church itself.* This institution, older than any university in the world, older than any government, older than any dynasty, exists wherever you have born-again Christian believers. Jesus said, "Where two or three come together in my name, there am I with them" (Matt. 18:20).

And this same Christ is the head of each church congregation, whatever its size, and He is the head of the whole Church. Paul says, "Christ is the head of the church, his body, of which he is the Savior" (Eph. 5:23). To the Colossians he wrote, "He is the head of the body, the church" (1:18).

The church, which Christ heads and in which He is always present, is so simple in its nature that a large number of participants is not required for it to exist. Its simplicity is stated in Acts where we read, "They [the people in the church] devoted themselves to the apostles' teaching and to the fellowship, to the breaking of bread and to prayer" (2:42). Here, the church consisted of (1) the apostles' teachings, (2) fellowship with each other, (3) the Lord's Supper, and (4) prayer. All that, of course, obtains in Christian congregations today wherever they may be—in large cities, in out-of-the-way towns, or in rural settings where they do not even enjoy a crossroads location.

This kind of church is not simply another institution of society, such as a school or a business enterprise. It is a *divine* institution. The church is not adequately described if we simply say that it is more important than any other social institution. It is really more than a social institution. It is one, and holy, and apostolically instituted, and theologically mysterious—divine, in a sense, like its Head. The church is also human, as Christ was. Actually, it is sometimes embarrassingly human.

The church, also, in its very nature, is unconquerable and conquering. Try to outlaw its existence as the Roman Empire did, or silence its witness, or change the allegiance of its members, and you have to feed some of them to lions, or drag them to their death behind your chariots—for it is unconquerable. Of this conquering host Jesus said, "I will build my church, and the gates of Hades will not overcome it" (Matt. 16:18).

This church, composed of local congregations in all shapes and sizes, which laud and applaud God in a thousand tongues, is one. That's right: it is *one*. The deceased persons in it are one with those living on God's earth now—like Francis of Assisi, for example, who was born 800 years ago in 1182.

41

He forsook wealth and pursued poverty and eschewed position and power to follow Christ.

Adam Clarke, too, of John Wesley's time, is one with each Christian in even the smallest church congregation. He learned many languages well, using them to write a commentary on the whole Bible. He pastored one congregation for 50 years.

Christians in out-of-the-way, pint-sized congregations are one with Christians who serve Christ in beautifully authentic and costly ways. They are one with the now late Rev. Jim McCloud, who was pastor for some 20 years in Greenock, Scotland. He and his 20 or so members were out-and-out Christians and the whole city knew it—in part from their frequent open-air meetings. During World War II Hitler's planes bombed Greenock frequently because many of Britain's ships were built there. During the bombings large crowds would rush to McCloud's church and kneel and pray on its steps. Brother McCloud's family had to leave, but he stayed and ministered. Dr. George Frame, his district superintendent, went to visit him and found him as happy as the proverbial lark, fixing himself a meal inside his bombed parsonage. Some of the walls were partially missing, and from the street the visitor could see Brother McCloud in his kitchen almost dancing around the stove in fulfilled happiness.

3. *Yet another basis for the significance of a small church congregation is that such groups participate in what might be called the "evangelical succession."* Roman Catholics and Anglicans have their apostolic succession in which they reckon that they have an unbroken lineage among their bishops back to the apostles. We, however, believe in an *evangelical* succession that each Christian and each evangelical congregation participates in. *This is the succession of those with new-made hearts, who have been justified and regenerated and*

42

reconciled and adopted into God's family as His redeemed children. In each new generation there must be and are enthusiastic rediscoverers of the life-transforming gospel experienced and taught by the New Testament apostles.

There is another aspect of the evangelical succession that each congregation of true Christians can proudly participate in: the apostolic mission of evangelism. Even as the New Testament apostles evangelized among the Jews and the Gentiles, so do evangelical Christians today as they testify of their faith among their neighbors. They too are disciples of Jesus Christ. They too are among His authentic witnesses. They too are fulfilling their evangelistic mission received from God through His inspired apostles.

If we Christians do this witnessing, some will receive the gospel and have their eternal destiny changed. When that happens to one person through the evangelism of a given congregation, and he matures in Christian faith, that service being rendered is of eternal import. Thus, since a ministry of eternal import happens even in the smallest congregations, such service is the most important kind of work that humans can enter into.

Conclusion

A number of years ago I was sitting at coffee with Dr. Harold A. Bosley in the church of which he was pastor—the large Evanston First Methodist, near Chicago. I was a young would-be theologian, and the two of us were waiting for the beginning of the opening session of the American Theological Society. Impressed, as a graduate of a Methodist university, with the fact that I was sitting in prestigious Evanston First with its pastor, I ventured the comment, "This is perhaps the most important pulpit in Methodism."

His response was made nearly three decades ago, but I recall it vividly—too vividly because it still stings. He responded, "Every pulpit is important." Both history and holy Scripture agree with Dr. Bosley, "Every pulpit is important," and every church where believers gather for a meeting with the living Christ is significant.

DISCUSSION QUESTIONS

1. Why do you think God reduced the size of Gideon's army? What must have gone through the minds of the 31,700 soldiers who were dismissed? the 300 who were asked to remain? Gideon?
2. The Bible never states whether the early churches were large or small. In your opinion, why didn't the writers of Scripture consider size to be important? Why, by contrast, do we place such a great emphasis on size?
3. Suggest ways that we may *think* and things that we might *do* to cultivate a deeper awareness of our oneness with all Christian brothers and sisters.
4. What is meant by the term *evangelical succession,* and what does this concept mean to you personally?
5. How can we begin to elevate the mission of the small congregation without downgrading that of the large one?

4

Big, Small, and Incomplete

by Dr. Paul M. Bassett

You have seen pictures of (or perhaps even visited) gigantic cathedrals like Notre Dame in Paris, Saint Peter's in Rome, or Saint Paul's in London. Very impressive indeed with their flying buttresses, massive stained-glass windows, towering crosses, and enough room to seat thousands.

After seeing such structures, maybe you've been tempted to say to yourself: "What a contrast to my little church back home. It is so plain, so small, and holds so few. To be a part of the throng that worships at a huge cathedral must be so much more uplifting and awesome."

But it is important to understand that the grandiose European cathedrals that so impress us were *not* built with size of congregation in mind. Their massiveness expresses instead any number of other thoughts: the splendor of the heavenly kingdom, the generosity of the benefactors, the depth of some donor's sorrow for sin and hope of forgiveness, the

DR. PAUL M. BASSETT
is associate professor of European Christianity at
the Nazarene Theological Seminary, Kansas City.
An ordained elder in the Church of the Nazarene, he has pastored in Ohio and North Carolina. He received his doctorate from Duke University, Durham, N.C.

importance of the relics housed under or near the high altar, etc. In no way were they meant to say something of numbers of believers—how many would worship there. The donors, builders, and users of those churches certainly knew the difference between large edifices and small, between large crowds and small. *But they did not translate relative numbers into relative spirituality.*

The fact is, throughout the history of Christianity those social units that we call congregations have considered themselves to be both *parts* and *wholes* at one and the same time—parts of wider Christian fellowships (denominations, orders, theological families, etc.) to which they owe accountability for faith and practice, and wholes because redemption in Christ is as complete over here as it is over there and the Spirit is as present here as over there. The Church Universal is the Body of Christ and so is each congregation within it. So the numerically small parish saw itself as one more fully authentic *colony* of the kingdom of heaven. Its size made no difference to it spiritually.

So strong and so ingrained was this idea in the mind of the Early Church that congregations said in confession of their faith, "I believe . . . in the Church Universal." The notion of "small church" as unique was associated with heresy, not orthodoxy. The very word for heresy carried the clue. It was *haeresis,* which by the time that the Church was taking its rise had come to mean "an exclusive body," a "clique," some sort of self-sufficient separatist group.

The Church used the term in just this way. In fact, for the Early Church heresy was as often a matter of party spirit as it was a matter of doctrinal error, as often a matter of too *exclusive loyalty* to one's immediate fellowship as it was a matter of *vagrant belief.* The worshiping community that did not reckon with its place in the Church Universal in its prayers and rites and instruction was on spiritually dangerous turf.

Now, having recognized these things, is it still possible to talk about "small church" in any way other than the quite superficial one that has to do with size? And, assuming that we can talk about it, does "small church" have a history?

The answer to both questions is a very guarded yes. The reason for this is that numerical size is not the only perspective from which we may develop a notion of "small church." We can think of *incompleteness,* of *deficiency.* We can legitimately refer to a church (congregation, order, movement, denomination) that lacks something that has historically been thought essential in its patterns of administration or worship as a "small church."

If we can think this way, we can keep ourselves in line with the historic understanding that each congregation is both a part and a whole. There are and have been groups of varying size and organizational complexity in which the whole gospel was at work who nonetheless recognized that they were absolutely dependent upon some other segments of the Church Universal for administrative or liturgical essentials. The means for recognizing dependence vary. And the intensity of recognition varies. But recognition is there, often half-forgotten in some ritual.

An example of this would be seen in the ordination of your minister. He cannot ordain himself. Ordination must be carried out by some representative of the Church Universal, someone representing a segment larger than your local segment. In fact, even congregations that are autonomous and ordain their own minister will not reordain a pastor who comes to them already ordained. Here is recognition of being both part and whole and thus being in some sense incomplete.

If we think consistently in this way, we must admit that *any* Christian group—congregation, denomination, association—is incomplete or deficient. And that is not at all an unhealthy perspective. But for the purposes of this book we are narrowing our focus so that we can consider the unique

47

circumstance of the numerically small modern congregation. Let us look at several examples of groups that were quite self-conscious of their incompleteness, to see what they can teach us.

I. Early Communal Monasticism

Do not let the heading scare you off. Those European monks 1,300 or 1,400 years back say something very important to today's small church—especially regarding the exercise of a spiritual "specialty." The usual Protestant and secular notion that monks sought only their own salvation is wrong. First, their culture had not developed the individualism that characterizes ours. For them it was thought necessary to be part of several groups in order to be truly human. Secondly, they thought of the Church as a society whose whole was greater than the sum of its parts; and outside of the Church, said they, there is no salvation. Coming into the Church was coming into a family; it was the family, especially Christ, the Head of the family, that gave you your true identity. The clear symbol of this is the fact that you were given a Christian name at baptism.

So even the nearly solitary monk knew that he was part of the Church and that the Church was necessary to him for salvation. This notion came to be expressed in practical terms very early in monasticism. The earliest idea was to go out into some wilderness area all alone to pray and to meditate. But these early hermits held such a good reputation for holiness and wisdom that people would flock to them for help and some would want to stay. As a result, communities sprang up and it became both necessary and spiritually healthy to see that these communities were able to allow for both solitary prayer and meditation and the sharing of spiritual insight.

Here the work of the Egyptian monk Pachomius (d. about 346), the Greek Bishop Basil of Caesarea (d. 379), and the Roman monk Benedict of Nursia (d. about 543), among others, made an incalculable contribution to the period. They would not let the specialists, no matter how holy, separate themselves from the Church at large. Their method was simple: they insisted on corporate worship, and as a part of corporate worship they insisted on the frequent celebration of the Eucharist.

This insistence underlined several points at once. Most important, Eucharist could not be celebrated without a priest, and since monks were most often not priests, it meant that a priest had to be brought in from a regular parish or from some other responsibility in the workaday church to celebrate this most sacred of Christian rites.

Then, too, in order to take part in the Communion, which is part of the Eucharist, one was expected to have made a good confession. This was done to a priest, who declared as a function of his priestly authority that the monk had been forgiven according to the promises of the Scripture to those who confess and repent. In addition to these things the prayers of the Eucharist were full of reminders of the whole Church—prayers for bishops in far-off places, prayers giving thanks for saints from all eras in Christian history, prayers asking blessing and divine aid for the Church in all the world.

Written into the very rules by which the monks lived, then, was deep awareness of their membership in the Church Universal, however useful and necessary their specialty might be. They needed the rest of the Church as much as the Church needed them. The value to the whole Church of a small, well-disciplined unit given to a spiritual specialty (in this case prayer) was not lost.

Of course its temptations were peculiar to it. Its very specialty could lead it to spiritual pride. Who could pray like a monk, after all? Who had the time and the skill? Monastic discipline could push into spiritual swaggering as well. Monks often mistook austerity for holiness—and the Church at large often thought that the monks were right and were the ideal. But these problems—this can be documented—were *worst* where the monastics ignored or overlooked or muted their relationship to the Church Universal and sought to be spiritually self-sufficient.

What early monasticism may say to the modern small church is a word about recognizing that *however small it is locally, it is part of the Church Universal and has the privilege of drawing upon those wider resources.* In fact it has a responsibility for bringing those resources to bear in its own situation. On the other hand, early communal monasticism may *encourage the small church to find and develop a spiritual specialty for the sake of the whole Church.* Unique temptations lie there, but there is clearly benefit for both the Church at large and the "specialists" if they will keep alive the interchange.

II. The Seventh-Century English Church

The English Church for the years 597-735 presented another path that the idea of incompletion or deficiency has followed. Here we will see an organizationally and liturgically incomplete Christian society at work transmitting a culture on behalf of the faith.

A very telling illustration of this sense of dependence and incompleteness and what it meant to the work of the English Church is seen in the tenure of Theodore of Tarsus as Archbishop of Canterbury. The man himself was 66 years old, of Syro-Greek origin with a relatively undistinguished career. From Pope Vitalian's perspective, Theodore's appointment was a move to buy time and was politically planned to ingratiate himself with the emperor in the hope of gaining control of the eastern wing of the Church. Obviously, the best interests of the English Church were not in the pope's mind.

And yet Theodore's 22-year reign is one of the most significant in the long history of Canterbury. Theodore's plan was simple: bring the English Church under willing obedience to Canterbury and place Canterbury obviously and permanently under the patronage of Rome. He also sought to undergird the English Church and peoples with a literary and material culture that would ground them firmly in the tradition of the Church Universal. Theodore succeeded on both counts.

One of his methods was to draw upon resources of the Great Tradition. He brought to the liturgy of the entire English Church the plainchant, so beloved in Rome. He taught his clergy Greek and Latin so that they might study the classics, Christian and pagan, and enrich the worship and thoughts of their own people.

Another of his ways of helping the English Church appreciate its incompleteness positively was to enter the English Church deliberately and concretely into the lives of the Church at large even on issues that were not pressing the English Church itself. For instance, at the Synod of Hatfield in 680 Theodore told the gathered English bishops of the theological battle in Constantinople over whether Christ had one will or two. The English bishops had little taste for any theological argument, let alone one so subtle. But Theodore argued that a problem of the Church Universal in Constantinople is a problem for the Church Universal in England. So the bishops declared their orthodoxy, probably understanding the need to be orthodox and part of the Church Universal better than they understood just what orthodoxy was at this point.

Another way in which Theodore helped the English Church to understand and capitalize on its deficiency or incompleteness was to help it to adapt Roman law instead of

Germanic law into its ethics and disciplinary procedures. His *Penitentiale*, a book of ethical, legal decisions, leans distinctly away from the strictly catch-as-catch-can, pragmatic, for-the-moment, personal judgments typical of Germanic law then. He relied on written law and systematic legal principle long established in the Graeco-Roman world.

During that same century English clerics scouted Europe for books, builders, and relics. All this was done in the hope of garnering sources for an English Church very conscious of its lack of them. Venerable Bede puts the account in writing in his *Ecclesiastical History of the English Nation*. He does not grovel. Rather, he delights in seeing that now the culturally and religiously deficient English have found a way to completion in the resources of the Church Universal. The doors of the English Church must ever be open to the Church at large, and out of the English Church must come unremitting care for the whole people of God.

What the history of the seventh-century English Church says to the modern small church is a word about *recognizing the possibility of drawing upon the resources of the Church Universal in order to educate its own people.* This story tells us that *numerical smallness need in no way portend intellectual or spiritual smallness.* In fact, if the intellectual and spiritual life of the small church be deep and broad, there is every possibility that it will contribute to the conversion of the culture around it. It was the experience of the seventh-century English Church that *it is the responsibility of the Church, no matter how weak or incomplete it may appear to be, to shape the culture, rather than to allow itself to be shaped by the culture.*

III. The Brethren and Sisters of the Common Life

Gerhard Groote (1340-84), a wealthy Dutch layperson, founded both the Brethren and the Sisters of the Common Life. Groote had been converted from the profligate life-style so typical of his social class. He accepted the ideal of imitating Christ—seeking to conform completely to the will of God (as it would be revealed through prayer and study), engaging in works of pious charity to neighbors, and surrendering any right to private possessions.

Groote gathered around himself a community of laypersons devoted to poverty, prayer, and charity. Other communities developed along the same lines and a movement was born. While the communities were concerned with disciplined living, they had little use for extreme asceticism. Rather, each member was to seek to grow spiritually through prayer, meditation, study, mutual confession of sins, and service to others. The aim was, of course, the imitation of Christ.

What is important for our task at hand is the way in which this religious movement of the 14th and 15th centuries recognized its organizational and liturgical incompleteness and turned it to good account for the sake of the Church Universal.

The fact that the vows of monastic orders bound one for life had led to some unworthy, if understandable, practices and attitudes. At one extreme were those who continually sought ways to interpret those vows in such ways as to permit them to do more or less as they pleased. At the other extreme were those who interpreted the vows so rigidly that they killed any sense of joy or self-confidence. The vows of the Brethren and Sisters were not binding for life, though it appears that the great majority taking them kept them through life. This voluntarism made the group most attractive in its joyfulness and seriousness of purpose. Here was *commitment without coercion.*

And, as a corollary, here was also commitment *without obvious community* at times. While the Brethren and Sisters did maintain convents, they also came and went and scattered singly and by twos and threes to teach in universities and work among the very poor and the ill. Yet, wherever they went they carried their deep piety and the strength of their commitment to each other and to the Church at large. They afforded the Church a model of piety as deeply spiritual as that of monasticism and as down to earth as any layperson could hope for.

Besides this, questions about their fidelity to orthodox faith fell silent. The Brethren and Sisters participated fully in the sacramental life of the Church—more fully than some, in fact, for they insisted that the sacraments were celebrated to no purpose if the believer lacked the inner spiritual disposition to celebrate authentically. Here was a refreshing breeze, for many a Christian tended to participate in mechanical or even superstitious ways. After all, official theology said that the performance of the act itself conferred grace. The Brethren and Sisters seldom criticized this dogma openly. Rather, they simply put weight on participating in the sacraments in *genuine faith.*

They seem not to have considered administrative or liturgical independence. Theirs would be a renewal movement fully loyal to the body whose renewal it sought. And not just loyal, it was to be actually *dependent* upon the body.

What the story of the Brethren and Sisters of the Common Life tells the small church today is encouraging. There is in North American society a tendency to believe that a small group makes its contribution primarily by a way of being a well-disciplined body. The Brethren and Sisters remind us that *far more important than discipline for discipline's sake is willing commitment to one another in such a way that the joy of the Lord is encouraged, not curtailed by the agreed-upon rigors.* Their story tells us that Christianity thrives best in the organizationally incomplete or liturgically deficient body when *commitment precedes discipline.*

In this way, the small church may become a model for the Church at large. As a small body, the small church clearly expresses its dependence upon the Church at large by its faithfulness in hearing the Word, in celebrating the great act of redemption in the sacraments and in faithful worship. In this way it confesses its need for the rest of the Church. But at the same time, it can, as no large body of Christians can, clearly express the basic Christian conviction that true spiritual community begins in disciplined personal commitment to Christ and to each other and not simply in loyalty to causes or institutions no matter how holy or high their purpose.

IV. Seventeenth-century Lutheran Pietism

In the 17th century we find an example of an incomplete or deficient group that recognizes its need for spiritual life beyond but through the required form and brings life to the Church at large. The example is called Pietism and it is found in two forms, one Calvinistic and the other Lutheran; the first primarily in the Netherlands, the latter in what is now East Germany. It is at the latter that we shall look.

Very few evangelical or Lutheran Christians in 17th-century Germany actively opposed piety. In fact most favored it even if they did not practice it. What they opposed was anything that looked like an attempt to save oneself by works instead of allowing God to do it by grace. And Pietism looked to them as though what they believed they must oppose. Pietism appeared to be a way of salvation by works. The problem was not piety but making an "ism" of it.

The principal founder of this piety-ism was Philip Jacob Spener (d. 1705), a prominent Lutheran pastor in Strassburg and Frankfurt. Spener looked back on his own adolescence as frivolous and was inclined to make the same judgment about much of the life that he saw swirling about him, though, perhaps surprisingly, he was not humorless. On the negative side Spener struggled against the moral carelessness and spiritual shabbiness of the clergy, the sterility of the worship of the Church, the superficiality of the laity, the aridity and pedantry of most theological education and discussion, and the meddling of the State in religious affairs.

But Spener was not content simply to find fault with things as they were. In his *Pia Desideria* (1675) he presented a positive program that quickly took root and changed the face of Lutheranism, especially in Germany, Scandinavia, and later, the United States. His first concern was to see people genuinely converted, to see them come into and develop a personal relationship with Christ that would issue in a holy life full of good works. To this end he gathered believers into "little churches in the Church" for Bible study, prayer, and mutual aid. Here he advocated a disciplined life-style, void of trivial behavior and vices such as card-playing. His idea was that while other doctrines were not to be discounted or discarded, only those bearing directly upon Christian living should receive major attention. And he developed a program for theological education that called for the personal conversion of each clergyman and for heavy doses of instruction in the practical side of pastoral life. The pastor was to be a model Christian as well as a wise and careful shepherd of the everyday life of his flock.

In none of this did Spener suggest that a new religious group be formed. He would seek to reform the Church from within normal channels and with instruments available to all. Only two generations after his death did any large number of Lutheran Pietists separate from the mother Church. This would have dismayed Spener. Otherwise he would have considered his reform a remarkable success.

Spener took pains to remind both his Pietists and his opposition that he had no intention of dividing German Lutheranism. And he worked, sometimes desperately, to avoid schism. His argument was that his "little churches within the Church" were finally not churches at all for they were not to engage in the preaching of the Word nor the administration of the sacraments on their own. These things were in the hands of the parish pastors and must not be arrogated or usurped. Of course one could hope to have a pastor of Pietist persuasion, but if the incumbent were not, he was still to be respected for his spiritual office. Word and sacrament could not be neglected nor bypassed. They were to form the very context of Bible study and holy living.

Spener's little groups and their descendants were sometimes spiritually arrogant and put many a pastor on the defensive. Yet where they were truly pious, they brought new life to a church nearly lost in its own theological pettiness and spiritual lethargy; they helped to revive a church that had become little more than a social institution, the State's department of morals and ethics.

Pietism faced two dangers. We have already mentioned one of them, the tendency toward self-righteousness on the part of the group. The other danger arose from the very concern for personal conversion. There was some tendency, and it grew, for the Pietist to think of religion as a solely individualistic matter, something between God and himself. The concern to study only those doctrines that bore directly upon Christian living tended to help the Pietists believe that other doctrines were absolutely unnecessary. They allowed the Pietist to believe that one or two doctrines could sum up the whole of Christian life.

But in spite of these temptations, tendencies, and difficulties the Pietists have something of value to say to the small church. Or maybe it is *because* of these temptations, tendencies, and problems that Pietism has something to say to the small church. So long as Pietism could fix its gaze upon its task of reviving the whole Church for the sake of Christ, it remained a vital, dynamic spiritual force in Protestantism. When it began to reflect in an egocentric way upon its own holiness and purity it became ingrown, arrogant, and unnecessary to the rest of the Church.

The lessons here for the small church are clear enough. Of course, it is not only the *small* church that has difficulties with spiritual pride. Large churches, too, can become instruments of the Evil One as they neglect to give praise to God for their marvelous successes.

But let us look at the positive side for a moment. Spener insisted that mature Christians lead his "little churches within the Church." Size was not to be mistaken for maturity. Nor was a small group ever to assume that it had less responsibility for maturity and spiritual life than a large one. The advantage of the small group was the intensity with which it could study the Scriptures and develop patterns for holy living. Added to this advantage was the fact that a small group could be more easily disciplined and be more easily directed to carry its message to the Church at large.

In a way, then, Pietism brings us full circle to early monasticism. Here is the smaller, administratively and liturgically incomplete society within the larger Church, exercising a "spiritual specialty." In the case of the Pietists, that spiritual specialty is much the same as it was in the case of the monastics: holiness of life, modeled. The chief difference between them is that monasticism moved in the direction of communalizing, while Pietism, sad to say, moved in the direction of an unwholesome individualism. At their best, both groups offer much for the small church to consider. And even at their worst, both point to the wiles of the Enemy, and say to the small church, "Here lies danger."

Part of the Whole

It is hoped that by means of this survey the small church has been helped to see both its assets and its liabilities. *Neither its assets nor its liabilities lie simply in the calculation and exploitation of its size.* In Christianity the idea of size as an indication of spirituality of any sort is a relatively new one.

As we have already indicated, each group within the Church at large was encouraged to understand itself as a *part of the whole.* Those groups in which the Word could be proclaimed and the Sacraments duly celebrated by appropriate persons were encouraged to think of themselves as small wholes within the larger body. In addition to these were what we might call para-church groups, groups that did not have license to proclaim the Word and celebrate the Sacraments without special arrangements with the hierarchy of the Church.

Today's small church must be seen from two perspectives. Very often its leader does have ecclesiastical license to preach the Word and to celebrate the Sacraments. From this perspective it should look upon itself as a small whole within the Church at large. But there is health as well in the small church considering itself to be administratively or liturgically deficient or incomplete. In this way it will incline itself to draw upon the resources of the larger Church, the Great Church. Also its dynamism will not be dependent upon its own resources of personnel and finances; rather its dynamism will lie with the Church at large. It is true that the large congregations and the Church at large owe something to the small church. But the examples with which we have dealt in this chapter have shown us that the small church, the organizationally or liturgically incomplete or deficient society, has a tremendous and varied contribution to make to the Church at large.

Maybe there is something applicable to the life of the small church in today's world in the words of the author of the Epistle to the Hebrews. The writer speaks of the great heroes of the faith and then says some surprising words about us: "These were all commended for their faith, yet none of them received what had been promised. God had planned something better for us so that only together with us would they be made perfect" (Heb. 11:39-40). It does not seem out of place to understand this passage to speak of the fact that *we really are dependent upon each other, large upon small, and small upon large.* There may be nothing spectacular about being small but, in the history of the Church, incompleteness and deficiency have often been avenues of the spectacular blessing and reviving of the whole Church.

DISCUSSION QUESTIONS

1. Explain this statement by the author, and relate your explanation to today's superchurch: "Those huge European cathedrals . . . that so impress us were not built with the size of congregation in mind."
2. What *two* meanings did the Early Church give to the term *heresy (haeresis)?* To what extent is today's small congregation in danger of falling into either of these traps?
3. To what degree should *any* Christian group—congregation, denomination, association—think of itself as:
    A. Complete?   B. Incomplete?
    (Can you recall any verses of Scripture to support your views?)
4. What important lessons can be learned by today's small congregation by referring to the following historical examples?
    A. Early Communal Monasticism
    B. Seventh-century English Church
    C. Brethren and Sisters of the Common Life
    D. Seventeenth-century Lutheran Pietism
5. In our day should large, middle-size and small churches increasingly see themselves as part of the one Body of Christ? Why or why not? If so suggest ideas to attain this goal without destroying local identity.

Three Worlds to Conquer

by Dr. Joseph Nielson and Prof. John Hawthorne

To be called by God to be His spokesperson is to be accorded the highest possible honor. What better way could the time and energy of one lifetime be spent?

Nevertheless, being pastor of any size church is no picnic. Someone has said: "A preacher has to be ready to preach, pray, or die at a moment's notice." In spite of any misconception that a pastor does not work—except when he

---

DR. JOSEPH F. NIELSON,
an ordained elder in the Church of the Nazarene, has been a professor at Olivet Nazarene College, Kankakee, Ill., since 1969. Currently chairman of the Division of Social Sciences, Dr. Nielson has written for numerous publications, authored several books, and is listed in *Who's Who in the Midwest.*

JOHN W. HAWTHORNE
has been an assistant professor of sociology at Olivet Nazarene College, Kankakee, Ill., since 1981. In addition to his work with the Association of Nazarene Sociologists of Religion, Mr. Hawthorne has taken part in a study of the holiness ethic of students at Nazarene colleges.

preaches his sermons each week—it must be admitted that his task is extremely complex and demanding. His duties are often unspecified, not very visible to most laypersons, and carry the weight of Divine expectation.

Being pastor of a small congregation is especially challenging. People are apt to be underwhelmed by his importance, his salary is likely to be inadequate, and he is usually without supporting staff. But none of these limitations lessens the pastor's desire to succeed—for God, for his congregation, for the denomination, for his family, for himself.

In this chapter we will examine three worlds to which the pastor must relate. In addition, we will examine the unique challenges and opportunities that exist within each of these worlds.

The pastor finds his life involved in three environments: *external*, *internal*, and *inward*. These worlds can best be thought of as a set of three concentric circles (see the diagram below). The largest circle is the *external* environment, which is the community. Inside this circle is the *internal* environment, which is the congregation. The *inward* environment is in the center. It forms the core of who the pastor perceives himself to be.

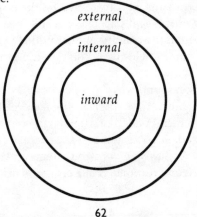

Now it is to be understood that the three environments are not to be thought of as isolated. Like parts of the human body they have a profound impact on one another—as they combine to make up the small church pastor's sphere of influence. Thus the pastor *must* be effective in all three areas. To be weak in one is to have real difficulty in the other two.

External Environment: Looking Out to the Community

Rev. Emerson was appointed to a church of 25 members. Its attendance had never exceeded 150. As he began his ministry the community was absorbing an inflow of Spanish-speaking people. In addition, the reputation of the church was at an all-time low due to some persisting internal church problems. It seemed an almost hopeless situation. However, with some idealism and plenty of faith he committed himself to ministering in this suburb.

To begin with he joined the Rotary Club and became acquainted with the local business people. Then things started to happen. He was asked to be the chaplain of the fire and police departments. Shortly thereafter the hospital director asked if the nurses and staff could enroll their children in his day-care center. It was not long before his fellow Rotarians requested him to help them relate to the Mexican newcomers.

Rev. Emerson found ways to minister to the community. As a result his church took on new life. It never became extremely large in membership or attendance, but an effective ministry emerged. A good number of people accepted Jesus as their Savior. And this all occurred after a creative servant of Christ located and responded to need-gaps in his community.

1. *Appraising the Needs*

The first lesson to be learned from this example is that it is important for the minister of the small congregation to develop a clear understanding of the needs of his community. One way this can be done is through trial and error, or trying a variety of approaches in the hope of eventually locating needs. Another is by interviewing community leaders. Still another is by locating agencies that provide such information.[1] Regardless of the method chosen, it is hoped that the congregation will not try to determine what the community's need-gaps are without somehow contacting the community itself. In Rev. Emerson's case, his relationship to the Rotary Club allowed him to discover much information about the needs of his area.

2. *Meeting Needs*

Once the community's needs have been identified, the congregation must determine *which* of those needs they should try to meet. After much thought and prayer, the focus must be narrowed. Trying to respond to too many needs can only bring failure and frustration.

Becoming aware of, and responding to, community needs is sure to result in a real sense of mission and purpose. With this in mind, the pastor of even the smallest church must involve himself and his congregation in bridging crucial need-gaps that exist—whether they be broken families, poverty, sickness, fear, or spiritual depravity.

In accomplishing this important task, Rom. 12:2 offers the pastor two suggestions. First, he must constantly renew his own mind or cultivate an awareness of God's presence in his life. Devotional life must not be neglected, for herein he gains his strength. Secondly, as his strength multiplies, he will increasingly "prove [demonstrate, or lead in the direction of] what is the *good*, and *acceptable*, and *perfect*, will of God."

We might diagram this admonition in the following way:

G = good (moral toward others)

A = acceptable (aligned with God's purposes)

P = perfect (holy within ourselves)

In summary, one of the pastor's primary tasks is to lead his congregation in filling the need-gaps of the community—with the good, acceptable, and perfect will of God. This is not an easy task, but one in which our Heavenly Father promises to provide strength and guidance (Rom. 11:36).

Internal Environment: Looking Around the Congregation

When examining the *internal* environment of the small church pastor, two points are worthy of careful consideration. First, he must obtain a steady flow of information from the congregation related to (1) their specific *expectations* of him, and (2) their *evaluation* of his performance as their leader. Secondly, he must continually analyze the internal organization of his congregation—with special attention given to the matter of *leadership*.

1. *Finding Yourself*

One of the most important tasks for the minister is defining his role in the congregation. This involves more than a "heart-to-heart" talk during the pastoral interview. There is an important difference between the *official* job description of the pastor and what his people expect of him.[2]

"I wish Pastor Green would preach more fiery sermons." "I like Pastor Green, but I wish he wouldn't rely so much on emotion when he preaches."

Pastor Green has a difficult time trying to satisfy both of these church members. Nevertheless, he must make himself aware of their viewpoints *and* their spiritual progress. And in acquiring this information he must be prepared to take the initiative and to resist the ever-present temptation to be either sensitive or defensive.

One pastor attempted to get a reading on his own effectiveness by distributing a yearly survey. Instead of asking for opinions regarding himself, he asked questions related to the deepening of their Christian walk. For example: *Are you spending more time in prayer this year? Do you find it easier to share Christ with your neighbor?*

In turn, this pastor measured his own success (in part) by the responses. Another pastor sought to obtain honest feedback from people who had ceased attending. And in so doing he obtained helpful information to be used for making needed midcourse corrections.

The pastor of a smaller church is in a unique position to be more keenly aware of the wide range of expectations that the members place upon him. Due to the more intimate nature created by its smaller size, the members tend to feel much freer to let the minister know what they anticipate from him and whether or not those expectations are being met.

Some pastors try to please everybody or become "all things to all men." Besides being exhausting, this approach leads to a dead end. Eventually a situation arises in which pleasing all parties is impossible. For example, a minister cannot be at a board meeting and in a hospital room at the same time. Another common approach is to back off from those demands that seem to have conflict potential. Mrs. Jones told her pastor: "You must not spend so much time calling on visitors and, instead, call on those of us who pay the bills." The pastor, sensing that others might feel the same way, responded to the demand by curtailing his calling on newcomers. It is easy to see how this "squeaky-wheel-gets-the-grease" strategy is doomed. To give a disproportionate amount of attention to those who scream loudest is to neglect the needs of the less vocal.

Conflicting situations must be lovingly faced head-on. The most positive solution to the problem of the minister's role involves the development of affirmative dialogue whereby pastor and laymen come to a common understanding of the pastor's ministry and the congregation's expectations. This calls for the pastor to work closely with the congregation, to understand what they think a pastor should do, and for the pastor to speak to the members about his view of his work. It is important to remember that the pastoral role is not inscribed in stone. It will (and should) change from time to time. And if pastor and people are continually involved in the process of helpful communication, they will be able to develop a clear understanding of the pastor-congregation relationship.

2. *Identifying Leaders*

Discovering where the leadership in the congregation lies is another important part of the internal environment of the pastor. Persons within the congregation must make decisions, and in so doing they become leaders. In some cases they may be on the official church board. However, in other instances they may not hold any formal position.

It is important to remember that there are at least two forms of leadership—*formal* and *informal*. The first relates to elected or appointed officials who are recognized by the organization; the second refers to influential persons outside of the organization's officialdom. These two types of leadership can come into conflict within the congregation. The policies and programs seen as important by the formal leadership may be quite different from those seen as crucial by the informal leadership.

What makes a person a leader? This can result from the individual's particular style of dealing with others, from social status, and from seniority or tradition. In fact, both formal and informal leaders may develop along *all* of these lines within the same congregation.

Some individuals in the congregation may become leaders because of admired personal characteristics. Because Sister Calhoun is very friendly with people, she may likely become a congregational leader. Hopefully she will be on the church board, but, even if not, she is still likely to make her influence felt. The successful minister will find a way to fit her leadership ability to some needed task in the church. In a smaller congregation, where there may not be a great variety of people with such leadership skills, it is even more important that the best use be made of those who have such expertise.

Leadership also comes from social status. Because Mr. Schwartz is an officer in the biggest bank in town, his social status in the outer world may transfer to the congregation. He is more likely to become a leader because people know he is important in the community. He may or may not have strong personal skills in leadership but is likely to wind up as an important person in the church nevertheless.

Some people may be church leaders because they have always been a church leader. This is the case of Mr. Wilson, who has been on the church board for years. It is likely that he will remain on the board until he is somehow prevented from doing so. Even if he is not reelected, he will remain a congregational leader simply because of his years of experience on the board. Another important facet of seniority may become evident when an individual is related to a family who has been in the church for years. Because May Lou belongs to the Brooks family, who were charter members of the church, she may always be an informal leader. Such a pattern is especially evident in a small congregation.

At times the pastor must cautiously remove, sidestep, or replace leaders who have risen to power. Much like a skilled surgeon, he must delicately correct the situation without damaging the healthy tissue of the body. Courage, patience, and understanding are essential qualities needed for this difficult but necessary assignment. Conversely, the pastor must nurture and train prospective leaders—as well as make their talents known to the congregation.

At some point dissension is likely to rear its head. But this is not necessarily a bad sign. In fact, in a very real sense such conflict is healthy. It is, no doubt, preferable to having a church with no diversity or conflict at all.

The pastor of a smaller congregation may have an advantage in dealing with the problems of formal and informal leadership because he can keep closer tabs on the congregation. The congregation can also help by being aware of the potential for dissension and by working to create an atmosphere of cooperation within the congregation. That is sure to lessen the likelihood that such problems will get out of hand.

Inward Environment: Looking Within Himself

Developing the *inward* environment of the pastor is the key to balancing the external and internal environments. If the pastor can develop inner resources to provide him a sense of stability, then crises in the other environments will not seem so drastic.

The pastor of the small congregation may find himself with few people to turn to when things seem tough. As a result he must learn the skills of introspection. He must learn how to "look within himself" to find the resources to help him through the rough times that come.

These inward resources involve such things as the pastor's self-concept, emotional temperament, concept of the ministry, and sense of mission. For the pastor of the smaller congregation these resources become vital. They allow him to operate in a situation that the world may define as undesirable without losing his zest for his ministry. If he has a strong sense of mission, a strong self-concept, and a clear concept of ministry, he will be effective regardless of the impact of the other environments.

Using these inward resources provides a mechanism for dealing with the varied demands and pressures of clergy life. If that can be done, the pastor will be encouraged, the congregation will be strengthened (spiritually and numerically), and the community will be served.

Victory

The pastor of a smaller congregation finds himself having to deal with a variety of situations. He not only has to successfully relate to people in his congregation, but he must find a way to deal effectively with those outside his flock: community leaders, social agencies, and the unchurched. While doing this, he must stay true to his inner conviction of what he represents.

Three worlds to conquer! Each crucial to the mastery of the others. To neglect one is to fail in all three. But in spite of the formidable challenge the minister of the small church must forever remind himself of God's ever-present concern and guidance. And that "plus" is enough to ensure victory. Victory in seeing people reconciled to our Heavenly Father and to one another! Victory in helping the pastor to measure up to the great honor of his calling!

DISCUSSION QUESTIONS

1. What are the needs in your community?
2. Which of these needs could your congregation best meet?
3. What can be done in your church to help pastor and people agree on the pastor's role?
4. How might leaders be developed in the congregation?
5. What would best help the pastor in dealing with pressures of the three environments?

   A. External   B. Internal   C. Inward

6

Opportunity in Community

by Dr. Richard Stellway

Recently I served on a committee that asked some people why they had stopped coming to our church. The responses went something like this:

Middle-aged lady: "My husband deserted me and our three children. We were emotionally shattered and financially demolished. Simply too embarrassed to go to church in our poor peoples' clothes—only to be asked painful questions."

Father of three: "My kids complained that they couldn't make any friends at your church. Since they didn't fit in, our family stopped attending."

Young college student: "I felt the church didn't challenge me. As a result I became bored."

Wear Your C.A.P.!

Why did these people drop out? In brief, they all thought that either they were not *accepted* or they were unable to

---

DR. RICHARD J. STELLWAY
has held positions at five colleges and universities. Currently he is teaching at Northwest Nazarene College, Nampa, Ida. His research and writing interests include the sociology of the family, the sociology of religion, and the third world.

participate in a meaningful way. To put it another way, they lacked C.A.P. (*Community Acceptance* and *Participation*).

Does your church have C.A.P.? Are people drawn into the warm circle of acceptance and participation right away, or must newcomers (and even new converts) undergo a waiting period? Are new people placed on informal probation, in which they must "prove" their commitment to God and desirability to the church?

1. *Community Acceptance*

Secular organizations have much to teach church laypersons about *community acceptance*. Visit an Alcoholics Anonymous, Amway, or Weight Watchers' meeting—or even a neighborhood garden club. Sense how worthwhile you are made to feel right off the bat. If you're not careful, you'll find yourself joining by the end of the first meeting. Plenty of C.A.P. at these places!

Have you been stopped by an Eastern religion cultist lately? If so, you were probably complimented, smiled at, agreed with, and given a gift of some sort—all within the first five minutes of your encounter. It's almost like the enthusiast says to you: "My life was incomplete until you came along." An excessive flow of acceptance gushes forth, along with a heavy dose of deception. If you're not careful, you can be "hooked."

Of all organizations on earth, God's church *must* offer total and sincere acceptance to people who are (or who feel they are) on the outside looking in. Christian laypersons must echo our Lord's admonition: "Come . . . all you who are weary and burdened and [receive] . . . rest" (Matt. 11:28). And when they come, they must *not* be seen as intruders trying to "crash our party." They must be given more than an arm's-length welcome and a first-timer's flower. Instead, they must be offered true *acceptance*.

Rev. Bill Sullivan put it well when he declared: "Today people are not simply looking for a friendly church, they're looking for a friend." They must feel wanted, needed, loved, admired, and affirmed—from the first moment of their initial visit.

Such acceptance is especially necessary today, when people feel restless and displaced. One in five families change residence each year; one in three children are from single-parent homes. Computers and telephone switchboards make people feel powerless. The result is stress, confusion, and loneliness. But accompanying these feelings is a deep longing for relationships with others who truly care—and who are able to communicate real understanding and compassion.

We Christian laypersons *are* that people. Our message is simple, direct, and powerful. Our love is genuine—with a bond that is eternal. Our mission is clear, as we follow the One who knew no stranger and withheld no help. The One who never hesitated to offer loving and total acceptance. Claiming to be His disciples, can we allow ourselves to settle for less?

2. *Participation*

The "P" in C.A.P. refers to *participation* or involvement. Christian laypersons, especially in the small congregation, must joyfully "own" chunks of responsibility. In short, they must realize that *they are* the church.

After the completion of a building project, or when things are clipping along smoothly (thanks to an efficient pastor and/or church leaders), there is a strong temptation for laypersons to lull themselves into a state of crippling passivity.

Even when laypersons are involved, they often restrict themselves to *maintenance-type* activities—duties that exclusively relate to keeping the church doors open. Here are a few examples:

landscaping	record keeping
secretarial duties	raising money
committee or board work	ushering
custodial services	program development

This is *not* to say that such activities should be neglected or considered unimportant. Weeds must be cut, committees must plan, records must be kept, and parishioners must be ushered to their places. Nevertheless, it is appropriate and even necessary to ask several questions.

Why should more than 90 percent of laity time, energy, and financial resources be appropriated to maintenance?

Couldn't at least 50 percent be directed toward *mission*—activities directly related to winning lost persons (outside of the church) to a saving knowledge and experience of Jesus Christ? A list of such activities might include:

calling on prospects	home Bible studies
ministry to conva-	with outsiders
lescent homes	hospital visitation
street witnessing	rescue mission (in-
prison evangelism	ner city) work
"cup of cold water"	canvassing for a
ministries; i.e., meet-	revival or spe-
ing physical needs	cial evangelistic
in the name of Jesus	service

My point is this: Of the laypersons who are hard at work, *most* spend *most* of their time and attention on the internal needs of the church. At the end of the year, their only satisfaction is in saying to themselves: "Well, we kept the old ship afloat another year!" Still more laypersons are underinvolved or uninvolved.

The key question is: "Why have we allowed ourselves to relegate mission-related activities to a place of secondary importance?"

Several reasons might be suggested, but I will confine myself to only two. First, maintenance is always easier than mission because it is less threatening. There is far less uncertainty involved and therefore less risk. It is always less demanding to do things for and with the home crowd—on home territory—than for or with total strangers. The latter are more likely to be discourteous or rejecting. Why increase the chance for such trauma?

I can imagine what would happen if we were firemen, and adopted this "play-it-safe" philosophy on the job. The alarm would sound, but we would volunteer to remain at the station—tidying up the kitchen, shining the pole, sweeping the walkway. Anything but going out to face the flames and danger. After all, our very safety and comfort is at stake—and the pole does need shining!

A second reason for adopting the maintenance viewpoint relates to our concept of ministry. For some reason we have developed the notion that ministry is something that only clergy are involved with. But the Scriptures teach us that ministry is something that all ministers should do—and Christian laymen *are* ministers (Matt. 20:26-27; Eph. 5:1-2).

James L. Garlow, in his book titled *Partners in Ministry*, underscores this truth. Quoting Francis Ayers, he writes:

> You are a minister of Christ . . . if you are a baptized Christian, you are already a minister, whether you are ordained or not is immaterial. No matter how you react, the statement remains true. You may be surprised, alarmed, pleased, antagonized, suspicious, acquiescent, scornful, or enraged. Nevertheless you are a minister of Christ.[1]

This means that winning people to Christ must be the burning desire of *all* laity. It's too big a job to be left to preachers; they are a small minority in the kingdom of God. As Garlow declares: "Clergy are not the ministers. They are the trainers and enablers of lay ministers."[2] We laypersons, therefore, need no longer confine ourselves to merely maintaining the church operation. Our place is at the front line, fighting the fires of sin and destruction that threaten our world. To paraphrase Thomas Gillespi: "If clergy will move *over*, and laypersons will move *up*, then both will move *out* to ministry."[3]

One more thing. New laity need not go through a long, drawn-out period of probation before becoming full-fledged ministers. As Ayers said, participation in the enterprise of winning the lost can begin as soon as they have given their hearts to Jesus.

For some reason the new converts I have known have seemed to be aware of this fact—and have led the way in bringing outsiders to the foot of the Cross. Their example sometimes inspires some third-generation Christian "pole-polishers" to join in the challenge of authentic fire fighting!

Small Church C.A.P.: Good Size, Good Fit

With good reason some argue that small churches tend to be more clannish and ingrown—thus, less accepting of newcomers. Especially when such newcomers show an interest in sharing "their" responsibilities.

To use an analogy, although the old-timers don't mind allowing the "new kid on the block" into the neighborhood, they aren't about to give him the secret password to enter their clubhouse. They must first be convinced of his worth and loyalty.

Few social scientists would attempt to deny this conclusion. Little churches are typically cohesive, traditional, and more resentful of newcomers. In a word, C.A.P. isn't usually dished out to them on a silver platter—as it seems to be done in multistaffed, multistoried, and multidimensional churches.

Nevertheless, an important point must be made. *If* small congregations once overcome this temptation to which they are inclined; *if* they can refrain from seeing "red flags" whenever outsiders draw nigh; then, authentic community acceptance and participation can result. And soon thereafter they'll be pleasantly surprised to discover that they're in an even better structural position to offer C.A.P. than larger churches. How is this so?

1. *Making Decisions*

The decision-making process of large churches typically rests on the shoulders of lay representatives. Such representatives infrequently consult the average pew-sitter for feedback before deciding on an issue. Logistically, to do so would be cumbersome.

By contrast, smaller congregations can more readily govern themselves in a democratic fashion. This means that laity in a small congregation are structurally in a better position to be aware of issues and to participate in their governance.

In short, small churches can provide more acceptance of laity opinion within their decision-making apparatus. More opportunity for involvement. More likelihood for having a say-so. Opinions and positions can be readily voiced, and by a larger percentage of people. As a rule laypersons can know what goes on and participate in decision-making and implementation.

2. *Doing Work*

On paper, large churches have a greater pool of laypersons from which to draw leadership. And it only stands to reason that the more talented persons would prefer to congregate in bigger ecclesiastical bodies. Good musicians enjoy the excellent instruments and superior acoustics. Top-notch Christian life workers delight in the creative programs and imaginative materials made possible by a paid ministerial staff.

Nevertheless, it is necessary to consider additional facts. The lay leaders of large churches, be they ever so outstanding, are typically few in number and often thickly spread. Reason: other less talented laypersons shy away from responsibilities because they see themselves as "not talented enough" by comparison. What average Joe wants to sing a solo after a golden-voiced virtuoso has just mesmerized the crowd?

To supplement the shortage of workers, large churches often resort to hiring professionals. However, this only causes the average layperson to shrink back farther. Two attitudes emerge. First, some laity ask: "Why should I try to compete with those guys?" Second, other laypersons assert: "It's not fair to be a participant and not get paid like those other persons."

Likewise, in smaller churches, there are plenty of opportunities for service. But often money is scarcer, worship tastes are simpler, and "participation rather than perfection" is the rule.

With this in mind, it can be assumed that smaller churches are structured to offer ample opportunity for on-the-job leadership training and meaningful responsibility. Laypersons with even a partial willingness are put to work. And when they become involved, everyone sees the result of their labors.

The resultant feeling in such churches is: "We're all in it together, trying to do our part, and learning all the time. Individually we may not be much, but together we are making a real contribution to the Kingdom."

3. *Experiencing Worship*

To paraphrase Rev. Albert Campbell, pastor of Mount Carmel Baptist Church in Philadelphia: "When people in large churches worship, the minister and choir are the performers and the congregation is the audience. But when people in small churches worship, the minister and choir are promoters, the congregation is the performer, and God is the audience."

As a rule, the congregations in large churches tend to resemble an audience. Many people in the pews are often strangers to one another, as they would be at a concert or a ball game. There is also the temptation to be a spectator—to sit back and be entertained. Frequently the emphasis is on *who* is providing the entertainment.

By contrast, at a smaller church the main attraction is meeting with God's people. Though there may be a lack of polished performers, the worship service typically involves active and enthusiastic participation on the part of the laity. And usually such active participation is "spontaneous." Sister Smith just might rise to her feet, unannounced, and request that Brother Jones sing the second verse of "Amazing Grace"—in memory of her deceased mother.

Therefore, the smaller congregation is in a superior structural position to encourage active lay involvement in the worship service: spontaneous singing, personal testimony, public confession, shared prayer requests, conversational prayer. These and other spontaneous expressions are more likely to blossom forth in small congregations. And, as a result, the people feel closer and more intimate. A significant koinonia emerges; a solid network of support is felt.

4. *We Know Us*

"We had a good attendance today. Did you see the size of that crowd? Why, even the front pews were filled."

"You know, I didn't see Mrs. Barnes in church today. Come to think of it, Mrs. Olson's nephew wasn't there either. I wonder if he's had another asthma attack."

These contrasting remarks reveal different ways of taking attendance. In large churches, impressions are based on the number of seats occupied—on the *size* of the crowd. Consequently, when the Browns are absent from church, the chances are that no one will notice or inquire about their whereabouts.

In small congregations, however, attendance focuses on the *presence or absence* of individuals. People will not only acknowledge the Browns' absence, but they are also likely to know that they're out of town visiting relatives.

Because of the intense continuity of communication between persons in small churches, people tend to be more "in touch" with one another and with their life circumstances. If the Claytons are having financial difficulty due to Mr. Clayton's unemployment, it is likely that all the people will know and many will respond with assistance. Conversely, if this family belonged to a church of a thousand, probably few would hear about the situation and fewer still would help.

The network of social webbing is tightly woven in the typical small congregation. As a result, there is an unspoken, unwritten expectation that each layperson will be truly concerned about the welfare of every other layperson. In short, the feeling is: "I am my brother's keeper."

Making C.A.P. a Reality

Community acceptance and participation is important for the survival of every social group. And considering biblical instruction, it is *crucial* to the life and vitality of the church. Why? Because laypersons, old and new alike, must feel unified and involved—in mission as well as maintenance—in order to feel fulfilled. Also, outsiders must see that the church provides such an environment. Otherwise, they are unlikely to be drawn to either the community of believers or their Savior.

This is to say that within the church, the bride of Christ, C.A.P. is not optional! And whenever the church lacks C.A.P., it is really not the church as Christ envisioned it. The church must be completely open and a "beehive" of meaningful, reconciling activity, with all people serving on the basis of their spiritual gifts (1 Cor. 12:4-11) as well as existing needs (1 John 3:17).

With this in mind, smaller churches have unique opportunities to achieve C.A.P. We have not meant to imply that all larger churches fail to achieve C.A.P., nor that all small congregations automatically possess this necessary quality.

In both cases, churches must be willing to seek God's enabling wisdom, guidance, and help. Only then can the barriers to community acceptance and participation be destroyed. Only then can true worship and reconciliation begin.

The goal is achievable. And it is *especially* achievable in that tight-knit community of believers that are known as the small congregation!

DISCUSSION QUESTIONS

1. How have newcomers or visitors described your church? What efforts are routinely made to make them feel a part?
2. In what ways do people in your church have opportunity to register their opinions? How do people respond to those who have opinions different from their own?
3. Name some new programs or activities that have emerged in your church within the past year. How many people are *aware* of these programs and their outcome? How many were *involved* in their planning and execution?
4. Are children and young people given opportunity for meaningful participation in the life and ministry of the church? What about other categories of people (e.g., aged, singles, young marrieds)?
5. Are laypersons able to describe their ministries? How do laypeople support one another in their mutual ministries?
6. Are there consistent and creative efforts to win people to Jesus Christ on the part of the laypersons in your church? What percentage of the laypersons are truly involved? Of those involved, what percentage of their time and effort is directed toward mission? Maintenance?

7

Shoulder to Shoulder

by Dr. B. Edgar Johnson

This following chapter illustrates how one denomination responded to the challenge of the small church. It presents a developmental analysis covering 75 years of that denomination's history and explains the attitudes, relationships, and trends that have had a direct bearing on the small church.

Many historians have linked the Church of the Nazarene with the Great Evangelical Awakening of 18th-century Britain. Its nearer roots are in the Holiness Revival that was so much a part of the North American religious scene in the last half of the 19th century.

Dr. Phineas F. Bresee, founder of the Church of the Nazarene (and former pastor and district superintendent in the Methodist church), voiced the stated purpose of the new denomination thus: To proclaim the message of holiness

---

REV. B. EDGAR JOHNSON, D.D., is General Secretary of the Church of the Nazarene. Rev. Johnson pastored in California before his assignment in the denomination's International Headquarters in Kansas City. He has served as president of the Christian Holiness Association and vice-president of the Association of Statisticians of American Religious Bodies.

throughout the world, in the same measure that we have received it.[1]

At the official birthday of the Church of the Nazarene, October 13, 1908, the general attitude toward small churches was one of wholehearted acceptance. In fact they were the norm. Then, when several holiness groups unified into a single body, there were 228 churches with 10,414 church members. The average size membership was 46. And most of the buildings were far from being ostentatious—by necessity as well as by design. Many met in such places as abandoned theaters and storefront buildings.

The Early Years: 1908-41

The primacy of numerically small congregations continued throughout the first four decades of the denomination's history. Seen as the ideal way to spread the gospel, small churches spread like wildfire and existed, so it seemed, at every crossroads. It was a challenge to provide an ever-expanding number of trained clergy, for the demand was very high.

In focusing on these productive years, it is helpful to pinpoint several factors that seem to be related to the rapid growth. These are:

1. *Revivalism and evangelistic zeal.* There was a strong consensus that *every* member should share his religious experience with nonbelievers. Dr. Bresee emphatically declared that we are "debtors" to such persons who are outside of the boundaries of the Christian faith.

2. *Enthusiasm of a radically renewed lay ministry.* In a very real sense, each member considered himself to be a "minister," a "spokesperson for God."

3. *Great financial sacrifice.* In a day of less affluence members were called upon to give heavily of their means. How else could the financial obligations related to the new

meeting places be met? As one old-timer declared: "In those days, Nazarenes gave until it hurt. Then, they continued giving until it stopped hurting."

4. *Involvement in small-group devotional meetings.* Spiritual growth was systematically cultivated within intimate circles of caring Christians—commonly referred to as "cottage prayer meetings." In structure and purpose, these sessions were similar to John Wesley's class meetings of the 18th century. Often nonbelievers were invited, and not infrequently they were drawn to the acceptance of the gospel. And the warm, supporting fellowship of Christ's followers within the group helped the new convert become grounded in the faith. Also, much of the overflow of spiritual energy engendered in the meetings "spilled over" into the regular services of the church.

5. *Lack of emphasis on buildings.* The so-called edifice-complex was virtually unknown in these early days. People were much more likely to rally around winning the lost than around constructing a church building. Dr. Bresee had solemnly warned about building spectacular structures and, thereby, alienating the lost of the lower-class. These forefathers took the founder's admonition to heart.

In his book titled *Assimilating New Members,* Lyle E. Schaller speaks of the folly of "architectural evangelism." According to this well-known author, spectacular structures will not produce church growth; instead, often the opposite is true. He advises that a new building should never be constructed unless the growth of the congregation makes it an absolute necessity.[2]

6. *Accession of other churches.* Observing the above patterns and noting the remarkable growth within the denomination, other churches of like theological persuasion chose to unite with the Church of the Nazarene. Each of these churches pooled their unique qualities with those of the larger body, and as a result, all received benefit.

To those in the early years it seemed as though the small church was the best vehicle to accomplish the goals stated above. Therefore, even concern about expanded membership was secondary to the goal of starting new congregations. "Beachheads" must be established before full-scale assault can take place. Influence must be spread out. The visibility of the Church must extend to as many places as possible.

There is evidence that almost every local church, be it ever so small, was interested in extending its borders by "planting" new churches. Members were willingly, and even enthusiastically, relinquished by their home churches for this biblical purpose. Revival meetings were held in distant communities. "Branch" Sunday Schools were organized. People called, door-to-door, to get the word out concerning a newly organized effort. In short, churches were more likely to look outward to the fields of harvest than inward to the concerns of home.

In addition, evangelists, district superintendents, and pastors were heavily involved in starting new churches. They not only saw themselves as caretakers of what God had already given, but had a driving concern to see new works begun—so that God might manifest His power in even greater ways.

It was *everybody's* business to evangelize the lost and to organize them into churches for nurture and outreach. With this in mind it is understandable that people today often reflect on the early years of the Church for inspiration and direction. Their vision was sharply focused. Their conviction was resolute. Their contribution was great.

The Middle Years: 1942-1982

No one really knows when or where the superchurch syndrome began—with its emphasis on big buildings, high finance, and complex programming. Across the years, subtle changes led to gradual modifications in attitude toward the issue of church size. Let's examine some of the changes and the evolving attitude.

Evidence suggests that, within the decade of the '40s, people were thinking about the possible implications of the denomination's rapid growth. Dr. H. V. Miller, general superintendent, put the issue sharply in focus at the 1948 General Assembly.[3] His statement directly related to the matter of church size.

> The continued growth of our church is to be assumed. So far our history has been glorious in this regard and virtually unprecedented. But we should *not* fail to recognize the liabilities that are implied in this continued growth. Large bodies move slowly and often clumsily. A smaller group has the distinctive advantage of quick reaction and compactness. The larger body eventually sacrifices these inherent advantages for growth.
>
> One thing we can and should do is to discourage the development of too large churches and too large educational institutions. Our church was never geared for large local units. To try to change this ratio might be disastrous. The far preferable method would be to protect ourselves by discouraging the building of too many large individual groups and institutions. With our intense program that implies personal devotion and responsibility to the common cause, leadership cannot adequately direct units that are too large.
>
> Rather than to think in terms of churches of 500 and 1,000, we should think in terms of congregations [that grow to a maximum] of 150-300. We do not mean to be arbitrary in these figures, but rather illustrative. We can minister more effectively with a larger number of strategically located congregations of smaller size over a given metropolitan area than we could with one or two large centers. We must always keep our people close to leadership.
>
> Let us be careful that we do not fall prey to the bogie of bigness. Smaller and better units will eventually prove far more effective as tools for growth and will present far less dangers of spiritual and ethical disintegration.[4]

Dr. Miller's advice was (and is) timely. Rapid growth often makes a church vulnerable to the "bogie of bigness." And when this occurs, some unfortunate consequences can result—which, in turn, stifle rapid growth.

The Church of the Nazarene has by no means stopped growing during the past 40 years. By 1982 there were over 502,000 members in the United States and Canada—in 5,049 churches. And the growth rate in other world areas has even surpassed that in North America. That is certainly encouraging.

Nevertheless, the growth rate has not been as rapid as in the early years. The Church has barely kept up with the rate of population increase. And what is even more significant, except for areas outside of the United States and Canada, a decreasing percentage of new members are new converts to the faith. A large percentage are transfers from other churches or children of the members. Of course, the latter are not to be minimized. But at the same time, it must be realized that effectiveness in reaching the unchurched has diminished.

The issue of decreased growth rate has been recognized by the denomination, and many steps have been taken to accentuate outreach. What's more, programs have been instituted to help retain the members that we have. In our mobile world, dropouts are a problem for all churches.

But the key question is: During these past four decades, what has been the trend in regard to church size? The fact is that average membership has doubled since the birthday of the church, from 46 to slightly over 100. However, over half our churches in Canada and the United States have fewer than 75 members, while two-thirds are under 100 in membership. The 1982 statistics are as follows:[5]

Membership Size	Number of Churches	Percentage
0-74	2,783	55.2
75-99	606	12.0
100-199	1,091	21.6
200-399	446	8.8
400-999	114	2.3
1,000-upward	9	0.2

With so many small churches, how has our average membership grown to 100? Because so many churches have grown well beyond the 200 to 300 maximum size of our early years.

I do not regret that our churches have gained numerical strength. Many advantages are connected with this trend, among them: better facilities, more opportunity for specialized interest groups (e.g., youth, senior citizens), and increased financial strength.

However, what *is* of concern is the attitude related to small congregations that has seemed to gradually emerge. This attitude contains the following ideas:

1. In contrast to the early years, the denomination now gives more direction in the area of church planting and evangelizing strategy. The result: control of the home missions effort has passed on to the individual districts. In a sense, no longer is the starting of new churches *"everybody's* business."

2. It is believed that small churches are *not* ideal. At best, they are only necessary as a point of beginning. But, like babies, they *must* grow. And such growth is measured by statistics that must be continuously reported.

To not grow is to be regarded as blameworthy—as unhealthy. Because of this, the church directs a disproportionate amount of its programs and resources into making small churches into larger ones.

3. The model for success, presented to pastors and laypersons alike, is the big church. Its pastors should be mimicked; its materials should be used (even in preference to

denominational sources); its programs should be adopted by the smaller churches.

Ironically, many persons connected with superchurches feel quite uncomfortable with the kind of attention they receive. As none other, they are aware of their unique weaknesses and the inherent structural limitations of their complex operation. Many would prefer to be left alone. To not be copied or lauded. But in a day when size is vigorously applauded, they are pushed on the stage. There they stand under the intense heat and brightness of the denominational spotlight. Not a comfortable place to be!

To describe this attitude is *not* to maintain that the Church of the Nazarene has completely neglected the needs of the small church in recent years. Not at all. Cooperative ministries have been consistently maintained: world mission outreach, youth camps, pastors' and laymen's retreats, camp meetings, coordinated efforts in evangelism. These are only a few of the unified programs.

Small churches are much too numerous to be ignored. Their collective strength is greatly significant, as is their contribution. Besides, they are still in the majority.

Nevertheless, during these past 40 years small churches have succumbed to a less positive image. Their inherent value has been questioned. No longer are they elevated to the plateau of the ideal. Rather, their most highly regarded asset seems to be their potentiality for growth—to become what they aren't now—big. To fail to do this is to lose status within the denomination, self-respect, and perhaps even the right to remain in existence. Often nongrowing churches are merged with nearby congregations or disbanded.

The Present and Future Years: 1983—

In the two time periods described above, it is evident that the Church of the Nazarene has somewhat polarized in its attitude toward its small congregations. During the early years, such bodies were held in the highest esteem. In fact, they were the central focus of attention. Then, as the denomination became larger and the growth rate decreased, attention gradually shifted toward big churches. Small churches were increasingly encouraged to grow—in order to become big.

At the present time another shift in attitude is taking place. In recognizing the unlimited potential of small churches in God's kingdom, the Church of the Nazarene is becoming increasingly attentive to its needs. This is not to castigate superchurches, nor to sanctify the reality of smallness. Rather, this new attitude is a balanced perspective.

Although growth is still considered an important indicator of denominational health, it is recognized that some situations have more growth potential than others. And in situations where increased membership is very hard to achieve, the denomination is seeing the need for their continued presence in order to maintain a continuing witness. Even though evangelization is slow, proclamation must continue. Seeds for future growth should be planted.

As a result of becoming resensitized to the potential of small churches, the Church of the Nazarene has initiated some courageous and creative efforts. Let's look at a few examples.

1. The denomination has led the way in advocating the return of the responsibility for planting new congregations to the local churches. An ambitious program has been developed under the auspices of Church Extension Ministries.

The "Oregon Plan," which is a program of rapid multiplication of new churches, was developed by a group of innovative pastors in western Oregon. They were backed by the enthusiastic support of the district organization. As a result of their efforts more than 35 churches have been organized within the last three years. The program has drawn the attention of many denominations and has been adopted by other districts within the Church of the Nazarene.

2. In addition to the church planting emphasis, the denomination has shown an increasing interest in providing encouragement and guidance to small congregations that are already in existence. The office of Evangelism Ministries is giving increasing attention to this crucial matter. Such things as informative seminars, workshops for church officers, upgraded reading materials, and various means of encouragement have been of great assistance.

This same general office has also given expression of its concern for small churches by sponsoring the formation of the Association of Nazarene Sociologists of Religion (ANSR). The association of highly trained, dedicated churchmen are actively researching small congregations in order to provide a better understanding of their characteristics and special needs. This volume is their initial contribution to this particular area of concern.

These innovative approaches *are* beginning to make a significant contribution to the small churches of our denomination. It is hoped and anticipated that trends, like the ones described, can be maintained and accelerated. As this occurs the Church of the Nazarene will be strengthened and fulfilled in its mission.

Never Too Small

The crucial question that the Church of the Nazarene, or any church body, must answer is: When is a church too small? Allow me to provide my own answer by citing an instance related to my life.

In the early days of my ministry I served a small rural congregation. The district superintendent's only advice to me, upon accepting the assignment, was: "Just keep the church open." At one point in my ministry there I was tempted to be discouraged. The doors were open all right, but just barely. Few were attending and the outlook seemed bleak.

At my lowest point I wrote a letter to my father. It contained my innermost feelings of sadness and defeat—and the fact that only five persons had been in worship the previous Sunday.

His reply to me came rapidly. He expressed concern for my plight. But then he said something that penetrated to the depths of my heart. His reply was: "Let it never be asked how many were present, but what was done for those who came."

Even the rural or village church is *not* too small if it has a minister trained in theology, who is guided by the Holy Spirit, involved in a caring ministry, and engaged in training laypersons to become effectively involved in the Kingdom.

A church is *never* too small if it has a potential of people within a reasonable distance who have not accepted the gospel of Jesus Christ.

A church is *not* too small if it has members who are genuinely willing to share Christian love with their neighbors and to encourage newcomers to actively share in congregational life.

DISCUSSION QUESTIONS

1. In what ways are small churches particularly susceptible to the following:
   A. Revivalism and evangelistic zeal
   B. Enthusiasm of a radically renewed lay ministry
   C. Great financial sacrifice
   D. Involvement in small-group devotional meetings
   E. Lack of emphasis on buildings
2. Can you share instances when people have attempted "architectural evangelism"? What were the results? When can a new and enlarged building help a church? hurt a church?

3. What would it take, in your opinion, for people within the Church of the Nazarene to resurrect the concern for small churches that was present in the early years? If it were possible, would this be good or bad? Why?
4. How can small churches best help superchurches? How can superchurches best help small churches? How can a denomination best help both?
5. What is so encouraging about the "Oregon Plan"? Do you know about any other plans geared toward the planting of small congregations? If so, please share.
6. What is your honest opinion concerning the following statement made by General Superintendent H. V. Miller: "Let us be careful that we do not fall prey to the bogie of bigness. Smaller and better units will eventually prove far more effective as tools for growth and will present far less dangers of spiritual and ethical disintegration."

Keeping the Small Church Upbeat

by Rev. Jack Nash

Our congregation carries on its ministry in the shadow of three of the largest churches in southern California. One of these churches boasts of having 11,000 members, and the other two claim an average Sunday School attendance of 7,000 and 5,000 respectively.

In examining our community of almost 2 million persons, I have often wondered why there are three mammoth churches and almost none in the midsize range.

If you were to draw a graph to represent the churches in our San Fernando Valley, you would start at the top with these three churches, then, abruptly drop to a host of congregations with an attendance of 100 or less.

Since I have never encountered such a phenomenon in

REV. JACK W. NASH
pastors Northridge Community Church of the
Nazarene in Los Angeles. He graduated from Olivet Nazarene College, Kankakee, Ill., and Nazarene Theological Seminary, Kansas City, and has
taken graduate studies at Butler University, Indianapolis. Prior to his current pastorate, Rev. Nash pastored in Wisconsin, Nebraska, Illinois, and Hawaii.

all my years of ministry, I began searching for reasons for its existence.

In time several suggestions began to surface in my thinking. It is widely recognized that our area of metropolitan Los Angeles is composed of many people who earn a high income. As a result, the materialistic trappings of affluence are evident—fine cars, boats, campers, etc. Such prosperity gives the people an air of pseudosophistication—a feeling of independence, security, and confidence. It is little wonder that such people might search out a church that corresponds with their exalted feeling about themselves. A big church—with a big program. And filled to capacity with affluent persons like themselves.

At the same time, the people of our valley aren't entirely satisfied with where they live. When pressed on the issue, scores say such things as: "This is no place to raise a family. Life is simply too hectic. People are self-centered and unwilling to be your true friend. Everybody is preoccupied with earning money."

With such an attitude, many of our people plan to move away someday. For the past two years I have been quietly polling my congregation, asking them about their future in the Valley. Almost unanimously they admit planning to relocate someday—to the desert, to some quiet and attractive area in northern California, to the Midwest where they grew up. Anywhere—just away!

However, the simple fact is that few make the anticipated move. Usually by visiting that "dream location" and seeing that it is no panacea, or comparing their salaries in southern California with those elsewhere is enough to discourage people from making specific plans for a move. So the persons in our area who someday hope to move rarely end up moving. Nevertheless, the continual hope is enough to cause them to be *tentative* about making deep and lasting commitments—to others and to responsibilities. Such persons seek out a superchurch where they can become anonymous spectators. And what they are deprived of in the way of relationships and task-fulfillment, they seem to find in the hoopla, celebration, and entertainment of the huge church.

With these facts in mind, it is easy to see why people in the Valley cluster in superchurches. Incidently, to stay in one superchurch for any length of time becomes even too demanding for many. As a result, the mammoth churches end up playing a game of "evangelical musical chairs." The pastor of the largest of these churches has, by his own admission, a church constituency almost entirely drawn from other churches.

The question we ask ourselves in our midsize congregation is: "*How* do we maintain morale in the midst of the prevailing attitudes in our community?" After considerable evaluation I share with you some ideas that we have discovered concerning the crucial issue of morale.

What Is Morale?

I cannot describe morale as I would describe my automobile parked outside my office. I can't say it has dimensions or weight or mass, but I know what morale is. Morale is what inspires a football team on New Year's Day to compete for the number one position in the nation. Morale in the family is the mother and dad going together on the long-anticipated second honeymoon. Morale is David going to face Goliath because he knew who he was and what he was called to do.

I can't describe morale in detail, but I can recognize it in people and in organizations. In relationship to churches, morale relates to the quality of the *emotional climate* in which we minister. And how do we create a good climate in the small church? Allow me to suggest four possible ways to build such morale:

1. *Love where you are.* As the well-known saying goes, "Bloom where you are planted."
2. *Leave it in God's hands.* Lay aside any guilt you may have, then relinquish the results of your total situation to Him.
3. *Light up your dreams.* Keep a dream alive. Believe God for some great event in your church.
4. *Lead from strength.* The small church has some decided advantages. Build on these with confidence.

Love Where You Are

First of all, morale is found in the love that pastors and people have found in serving the church where they are.

Cecil Murphey said, "Part of my calling as a minister is to help provide an atmosphere where love happens."[1] We can paraphrase that to say: If small churches will cultivate love, morale will grow. People will anticipate great things. Visitors will be drawn to the fellowship. Unity of spirit will prevail. For as church growth consultant John Wimber has said: "People go to church for many reasons. They stay for *one.* Because they find a personal relationship with God and a bunch of people who love them very much."[2]

There is a church in our area that has averaged 45 in attendance for several years. They have a different group of people today than they did several years ago, simply because the people who have become converted have moved away. Meanwhile, others have moved into this community and found the Lord through the loving ministry of this church. Looking at the statistics, some might say: "That church hasn't grown." But that church *has* grown, because it has faithfully added converts to God's kingdom.

If the pastor and people can love one another and love their mission, a serious morale problem will not develop. To

97

love where you are is to take the first step in building a ful-filled and challenged congregation.

Leave It in God's Hands

In a recent interview noted pastor and author Charles Swindoll described a brokenness in his spirit that occurred during his first pastorate. The church was small, and the growth potential seemed nil. He declared: "The turnaround came when I realized that no matter what the result was, I am God's man and I answer only to Him."[3] This pastor learned early to leave his ministry in God's hands!

When I served as Duane Deaton's pastor, he was a young man in his 30s advancing rapidly in a very large corporation. Even at that young age he had a very responsible position and was offered lucrative promotions. The only problem was that if he took the promotions, he would have to move to another state. He prayed about it. Then he told his super-visors: "I appreciate your confidence in me, but I cannot ac-cept any promotion because I have a commitment to my church. I am happy serving in my church, and I feel that this is where God wants me." Those of you in corporate manage-ment know that he, in taking that stand, risked his position on the ladder of corporate advancement. Mr. Deaton relin-quished his career to God. In our present day of weak and fleeting commitment, I often recall Duane's stand and am encouraged.

Whether you are a pastor or a layman, there is no need to feel guilty about being a member of a small church. The best way to avoid this matter of low self-esteem or a feeling of guilt about being small is to leave the size of your church in God's hands. Commit the whole issue to Him (cf. Ps. 37:5).

Thank God for the large congregations. They are great resource centers for inspiration and training. They have the budgets and the personnel to lead out in many areas that are very important for the success of the church. Yet, Lyle Shaller brings us back to reality when he reminds us, "The normal size for Protestant congregations on the North American continent is one that has fewer than 40 people at worship on a typical Sunday morning."[4]

Too many of us are intimidated by the size of the super-churches and the power of the electric church. This is especially devastating when a well-meaning member comes to church on Sunday morning with a condescending attitude, having watched Oral Roberts, Robert Schuller, Jerry Falwell, and Rex Humbard. More than one pastor has considered throwing in the towel after hearing a parishioner drop star-studded names, recite dazzling exploits of million-dollar Sundays, and relate Miss America's glowing testimony. Merle Allison Johnson, in *How to Be Happy in the Non-Electric Church*, asks the TV Christian one very simple question: "If Rex doesn't preach your funeral, who will?"[5] That ought to inject a little humor in your ministry and bring both you and your intimidator back to reality very quickly.

Leave it all in God's hands and lay aside that guilt. To repeat, refuse to feel defeated or to have a low level of self-esteem about the ministry in your church. If God called you where you are, then you are important. Size is not the sole criterion for success. God wants to know if your church is alive—and is doing its best to grow in quantity and quality.

There is one word of caution I would leave for any church, small or large. God cannot bless any of us if we feel that His church is *our* vineyard. Jesus forever laid that idea to rest when He told the parable of the workers hired in the vineyard (Matt. 20:1-16). Some worked 12 hours, some worked 9 hours, some worked 6 hours, and some worked only 1 hour. Nevertheless, at the end of the day, all were paid the same wage. You will recall that those who worked longest and struggled hardest were resentful. How could the owner be so unfair as to pay those who worked only one hour a full day's salary?

If the small church has an Achilles' heel in its morale and its ministry, it is at this same point. Typically, the small congregation is filled with many courageous, sacrificial people who have worked hard and long. And if the latter are not careful, they will come to resent the stranger within the gate. They will start to resent the generosity of God in accepting and rewarding the one coming at the eleventh hour.

The only thing that will save us from such a self-destroying attitude is to remember that it is *not* our church, it is *not* our party (as the elder brother so wrongfully thought). It is *His* church and *His* party and *He* can invite anyone He desires. *He* is the owner of the vineyard. It will help us in our work to know that *His* vineyard extends around the entire world. We are in just one small section of it. So regardless of the size of our church we must work diligently for *His* glory and be grateful when *anyone*—at *any time*—joins us in our important task.

Light Up Your Dream

Lack of vision, or not having a dream, will kill the morale in any church, small or large. Keep a dream alive! There is great potential in even the smallest church. So no matter how small the church is, it can and must have a dream. Such a dream might begin in a pastor's mind and heart and then come to be shared by laymen. Or in some cases the laymen will have a dream that will inspire the pastor. The origin of the dream is not crucial, but the reality of its existence is.

I know about a church that today is very successful. They became that way because three laymen had a dream. These wonderful people met with their minister and said: "Pastor, we are at the point of extinction and we feel just as the four lepers did in the Old Testament who sat outside the city gate of the enemy and asked one another: 'Why stay here until we die?' (2 Kings 7:3). Likewise, if we are going to die, we are going to die trying. We are going to believe God for something great." And that congregation did accomplish something great—which all began with a dream.

There is another church that will never be big. The demographics of the area dictate that. They are in a rural area, but they have a dream. As a result they exceed almost every church in their denomination in per capita giving for missions. Because of that, they too have a high level of morale. We need a dream in every church. Each one, no matter how small, can excel at something.

It can safely be stated that church morale goes up or down in accordance with the way church leaders (clergy *and* laity) light up the dream God has given them. Why did Jesus keep talking about the kingdom of God and the kingdom of heaven? Why did He say, "My food . . . is to do the will of him who sent me"? (John 4:34). It was because He had a purpose, a dream. Why did He continue when even His disciples misunderstood and revealed shallow commitment? Why did He do that? Because He was compelled by the vision the Father had given Him.

Dreams are the "stuff" of morale building. On one occasion I asked a college professor of mine what should determine when a pastor should leave a church. He said very simply: "It is when you cease to dream; when you cease to have a vision for your church. That is the time to leave and not until then." At one time in my ministry a denominational leader told me: "There are times when you will be in a church and things will be going well and you will want to stay, and God will say, 'Leave.' There will be times when you will want to leave, and God will say, 'Stay.'" I have thought about that statement many times. If God says, "Stay," even in times of smallness and apparent difficulty, He will help us by implanting a dream and a vision for that church. A dream that can be fulfilled when we become partners with God.

Lead from Strength

If we are going to be happy about our church and enjoy ministering in it, regardless of its size, we must discover what it does well—and *do that* to the best of our God-given ability. Granted, it is impressive to offer a wide variety of ministries. Often people are attracted to a great number and variety of programs. There is, however, another way to make the church winsome. Dr. John Wimber, mentioned earlier, suggests that instead of trying to make the church into a "supermarket" and trying to supply everything, the small church should become a "specialty shop." He tells about small, poorly located restaurants that have limited means. Still, people drive many miles to get a good meal there. He describes how people will stop in small specialty shops in the shopping center because of good personalized service.

The small church has a distinct advantage. It is a great laboratory for building leadership through involvement. If a person really wants to be involved, there is no better place than in a small church.

Another strength of the small church is its ability to be flexible. In general it can be expected to respond more quickly than the large church. I would not compare the larger church to Goliath, nor say the small church is totally like David, but there are some interesting parallels. Had David tried to take on the huge armor of Saul and move against the bulky Goliath, he would have been defeated. He took the advantages that God gave him and won a great victory for Israel (1 Sam. 17:38-54).

The small church must lead from strength. But it must begin by discovering what those strengths are. Then, they can be honed to a high level of perfection. Just as David may have had less armor and less mass than Goliath, he also had the advantage of having practiced his slingshot art to a fine degree.

The smallest church can and must have *at least* one strong ministry. It might be directed toward the parents of a Christian day school, the children of a church scout troop, the senior citizens of a convalescent home, or the divorced singles of our fragmented society. As a church discovers and develops its God-given strengths, it will begin to experience its God-given potential. And that results in a sense of true fulfillment and authentic mission.

Morale Can Be Anywhere

It's a simple formula, really. If we *love* where we are, *leave* it in God's hands, *light* up our dreams, and *lead* from our strengths, we will have high morale. In a sense, morale is not something for which we should aspire. Instead, it is a result of paying the price—of meeting the necessary conditions.

High morale occurs in all sorts of environments. Victor Frankl cultivated it in a repressive Nazi prison camp. Helen Keller grasped it in the midst of blindness. Paul found it after a shipwreck. Jesus seized it on a lonely mountain, as His saddened heart communed with His Father.

And *we* can have high morale in small congregations, whether they be at mission stations in Africa, house churches in China, chapels on military bases, or churches in small villages. The size or place of such gatherings is really of little consequence. For morale is measured in qualitative, not quantitative terms.

DISCUSSION QUESTIONS

1. How do you define *morale?* What evidences of it (low or high) do you see around you?
2. What characteristics of your city or community might possibly lower the morale of your church? What steps are (or could) you take not to let this happen?
3. What are some results of poor morale in a small church? high morale?
4. In what ways does your church:
   - A. Love where they are?
   - B. Leave it in God's hands?
   - C. Light up your dreams?
   - D. Lead from strength?

   In what specific ways might improvement come in each of these four vital areas?
5. How can small churches today successfully compete with super-churches and television ministries?
6. What "specialty" or specific strength have you observed in small churches that you have known about? How about in your own church?

9

The Little Church That Could

by Kenneth E. Crow

They stood in the church parking lot discussing the lack of growth in their congregation.

"Our church doesn't grow because it doesn't do what it takes to grow!"

"We aren't growing because our pastor has so little vision and ability."

"Laymen in our small congregation are comfortable and carnal. If they wanted their congregation to grow, it would grow."

Like the subjects of weather and politics it seems like everyone is a self-avowed expert on the topic of church growth. And when concerned Christians get together these days this very subject often arises. Both pastors and laymen are eager to be responsible Christians. Perhaps, especially in

---

REV. KENNETH E. CROW, doctoral candidate at the University of Colorado, Boulder, Colo., is assistant professor of sociology at Mid-America Nazarene College, Olathe, Kans. Prior to this assignment, he served as a missionary and pastor in the Church of the Nazarene. As a missionary, he applied church growth theories to small African congregations. While pastoring in the United States, he transferred church growth principles from theory to practice.

5

small congregations, there is a deep concern that the church fulfill its mission.

However, the kind of instant analysis above, in which concerned Christians make accusations, is generally frustrating and largely unproductive. Something more helpful is needed. The church growth movement and current church research are beginning to provide that help for small as well as large congregations.

One church growth authority has said, "The indispensable condition for a growing church is that it wants to grow and is willing to pay the price for growth."[1] With rare exceptions, *any* congregation can grow. However, *both* pastor and laity must want their congregation to grow and *both* must be willing to pay the price for growth.

This idea points us to the importance of four conditions for growth in small churches. *Desire* for growth in membership is a first necessary condition for growth. The other three conditions have to do with the cost of growth, which are:

1. Cost of similarity
2. Cost of closeness
3. Cost of usefulness

Put very simply, churches that grow must be similar to, close to, and useful for the people they are trying to reach.[2]

To Grow or Not to Grow

1. *The Dilemma*

The first important question each congregation must answer is: *Does our congregation, both pastor and people, really want to grow?* We know the right answer! Almost every pastor and layman will openly say they want their congregation to grow. However, often when new Christians begin to come in, the pastor or the members will provoke some crisis to prevent growth.

Sincere Christians will offer support for a new program to bring in new people, but a dispute will emerge over some policy or program. In the effort to settle the dispute, the new program will never quite get off the ground.[3]

This discrepancy between what we say and what we do is important. As is noted elsewhere in this book, there are real values to small congregations. Bigger is not necessarily better. And this fact is recognized by small churches. In fact one key reason why pastors and laymen of such churches fail to desire growth is that they know, at least intuitively, that growth will almost inevitably change the nature of the small congregation in terms of accountability, fellowship, and responsibility.[4] Undeniably, these are real values. Resistance to their loss is neither irrational nor unspiritual.

Two issues are included in this first question. The first is: *Do we sincerely want to be faithful to the Great Commission?* This is not the same question as the second issue: *Do we want to have a large congregation?* Making disciples does not necessarily imply making large congregations.

2. Obedience to the Great Commission

In response to the first issue, the church growth movement reminds us of the mission of the church. While there are options available to us concerning organization and arrangement of members, we do not have an option of whether or not to carry out the Great Commission. This is a mandate for every congregation. The command "Go and make disciples" (Matt. 28:19) does not fall away when a congregation reaches some optimum size. We must continue to win the lost.

If the issues of obeying the Great Commission and developing large congregations were considered separately, many small churches would answer yes to the first but no to the second. When this is the pattern of their answers, the discrepancy between what they do and what they say may be explained. For some there is an important conflict between these issues. However, it *is* possible to spread the gospel and maintain the advantages of the small group at the same time.

3. *Organizational Options*

Most small churches must begin the growth process within the congregation. The church growth movement calls such conversion and spiritual development of members "internal growth."

Some congregations may not expect much growth beyond internal growth. However, in all situations there are unsaved relatives and friends within the area who need evangelizing. And as evangelism is effective, additions will be made to the membership. But a dilemma eventually emerges. An influx of new converts is bound to present a problem for pastors and members who recognize the values of the small group—who want growth but not a large congregation.

Here is the good news: Values of the small congregation can be maintained while membership increases. How? By multiplication of congregations. Growth can be managed by planting new fellowships. What's more, this appears to be consistent with the pattern of the New Testament and the Early Church.

Other growing small churches will be able to preserve most of the values of their congregation by creating small groups within their structure that maintain the strengths of the former small church. The Wesleyan tradition of class meetings, or bands, provides one model of the rigorous commitment that would preserve accountability and intimacy within larger congregations. However, it should be recognized that this option is so difficult to achieve that it often fails to take place.

Small congregations may legitimately want to avoid becoming large churches. They may, therefore, organize their new converts in such ways as to preserve small congregation strengths. However, *no* church should curtail its desire to make disciples. Most small congregations will want to grow, to reach out in obedience to the One who issued the Great Commission.

This desire for outreach is a necessary condition for church growth. But it will not cause it. Congregations grow as they are willing to pay the costs for growth. Let us examine three:

The Costs for Growth

1. *The Cost of Similarity: Removing Barriers*
a. *Principle*

Anything that improves the fit between the congregation and its potential converts should improve growth. Anything that reduces the similarity between the congregation and the people for whom God has given it responsibility should be expected to limit growth or cause decline. To require people to become socially uncomfortable in order to receive the gospel limits growth. *Will our congregation seek to remove unnecessary social barriers between us and people in spiritual need?*

Of course some barriers are necessary. The prophetic voice of the church must not be compromised. The church must oppose and avoid the evil of our culture. This may well raise, rather than remove, barriers.

I remember trying to build a bridge from the congregation to a man who had a severe problem with alcohol. He laughingly told me of another pastor who had had a drink with him in his attempt to build such a bridge. The man was not impressed with the extent of the clergyman's willingness to become like him.

There are, however, unnecessary barriers. Small congregations that want to grow must pay the price of helping to erase the differences between the congregation and the people in need. This will not always be easy. There is a built-in tension between outreach and separation from the world. Denominational leader J. B. Chapman cautioned his own church that, "Denominations [tend to] either become in-growing movements or reach out and become diluted."[5] Our goal must be to avoid *both* traps—in denominations as well as small local churches.

b. Application

Within that tension, and without spiritual compromise, important adjustments are possible. These may be made in such areas as the social, the economic, the political, and the cultural aspects.

On the mission field where I served, similarity meant not asking Zulus to become fluent in English in order to hear the gospel. Missionaries like myself sought to improve cultural similarity by learning the language of the people. Admittedly, my use of Zulu never escaped the problem of a Nebraska accent.

Similarly, American congregations must find ways to reduce unnecessary economic, political, or educational divisions between themselves and potential converts. In the area of economics, Phineas F. Bresee (founder of the Church of the Nazarene) argued that fine and expensive church buildings tend "necessarily to drive the poor from the portals of the so-called house of the Lord." He said: "[I am] convinced that houses of worship should be plain and cheap, to save from financial burdens, and that everything should say 'welcome' to the poor."[6] He believed that elaborate buildings reduced the economic similarity between the congregation and the neighborhood it was trying to reach. The rule is: If buildings increase similarity, they can contribute to church growth; however, if they decrease similarity, they are likely to hinder growth.

c. Focus

Dr. Bresee's concern for the poor demonstrates the importance of *identifying* those groups for whom God has given us special responsibility. Without such identification, it would have been impossible for him to anticipate the effect of expensive buildings. He felt that the impoverished were the specific "near neighbors" to which church construction should adapt. Everyone in the community was welcome; however, it was the poor for whom Dr. Bresee felt a special responsibility. Having identified that responsibility, he planned a strategy geared to reaching this group.

In the parable of the good Samaritan, Jesus enlarged the definition of the neighbors for whom we are responsible to include *more* than geographical nearness. "Neighbor" means the person whom God gives us the opportunity and responsibility to serve (Luke 10:25-37). Congregations, like individuals, need to carefully identify these "neighbors" and serve their needs.

Most of us do not want to restrict the focus of our evangelism. We would like to provide enough variety to appeal not only to a single group, such as the poor, but to every group in the community. However, our resources are limited. This is especially true for small congregations. As we utilize those limited resources, choices must be made as to what will more likely improve similarity with the group or groups to which we feel a special responsibility or feel best equipped to serve.

Careful evaluation of the congregation's characteristics will provide one basis for determining God's direction in this regard. For example, the style of music that is enjoyed in the worship of the congregation will appeal to some, but certainly not all, groups within the community.

Congregations are socially as well as geographically located. Most converts come from among those people in the community who have significant social relationships with people who are already members. Therefore, the social characteristics of the most responsive groups will tend to be similar to those of the church.

A second method of identifying groups for whom God has given the congregation special responsibility is to analyze how God has already used the ministry of the congregation. As the congregation has served the community through the years, there has been a more positive response from some groups than from others. This backlog of experience provides some indication of the groups to which the congregation can more readily minister. Identifying these groups and improving congruity between them and the congregation should, in turn, result in growth.

2. *The Cost of Closeness: Reducing Distance*

a. *Principle*

The location and ministries of the local congregation must be accessible to people we are trying to win. When the location of the church is such that it is frustrating or inconvenient for potential converts to reach, growth is prevented or at least hindered. For example, as a rule, people are usually not willing to drive to a church that is farther away than the distance they normally drive to their daily activities. While the deeply committed member may be willing to drive much farther, potential converts will be much less likely to tolerate the inconvenience of a long distance.

b. *Importance of Location*

Obviously, some congregations are in locations where membership growth is more easily accomplished than in others. Many mistakenly assume that church actions alone prompt positive responses within the community. However, it is often the other way around. Community circumstances can also generate church growth. Along this line, a recent study underscores the importance of church location. Newman and Halverson found that, during the years 1952 through 1972, 44.9 percent of membership change in the Church of the Nazarene could be explained by such contextual factors as population growth, median age within the community, and median income in the community.[7] The location of the congregation *is* an important influence on growth. Granted, some situational causes of growth and decline are beyond the control of the church. There are, however, issues related to location that are well within the control of the congregation.

c. Application

Jesus instructed the church to be His witnesses "in Jerusalem, and in all Judea and Samaria, and to the ends of the earth" (Acts 1:8). One great congregation in Jerusalem would have been more convenient and exciting for the disciples. But Jesus commanded that the gospel be taken closer to the various groups in the world. We have followed those instructions by planting congregations in the ends of the earth. And God has honored His promise to us as we have applied the principle of closeness—making the church more accessible to people.

In the church planting strategy of the Christian community, large *and* small congregations have emerged side by side. Such a pattern has increased closeness. Super congregations provide a unique source of inspiration for all Christians. However, they can never achieve proximity to the many areas and groups we should serve. The small congregations take the gospel geographically closer to the needy. Thus, both large and small serve valuable, complementary functions.

Congregations must see their accessibility through the eyes of the groups for whom God has given them responsibility. When the facilities of the congregation are too inaccessible to achieve closeness between the church and potential converts, two options may be considered.

It is possible that the congregation should relocate. They may need to move closer to the people who look to them for ministry. In short, the question should be: *Where do we need to be located in order to be most conveniently available to the groups God is directing us to serve?*

On the other hand, it may be that the congregation needs to reconsider its understanding of near neighbors. It could be that God would have them refocus their ministry on the groups that are located geographically around the church. In this case the question should be: *What adjustments do we need to make in order to better serve the people that God has placed near our church?*

3. *The Cost of Usefulness: Serving Better*

a. *Principle*

There is one final area that has a major influence on growth. Anything that makes the church more useful to the potential members should result in growth. *Will our church pay the price of meeting the needs of our near neighbors?*

The most obvious and important area of congregational usefulness relates to the spiritual. When people are not having their spiritual needs met, they are more likely to look for another place to worship. But there are also other important needs that must be met by the small congregation if they are going to attract nonbelievers.

b. *Relationships*

The intimacy and accountability that large congregations often find difficult to provide are common to small churches. They are especially effective in meeting the need for social relationships. And small congregations that desire to grow will build on this inherent strength.

Relationships between present members and potential converts are especially crucial. This is demonstrated in the results of two recent studies. Stark and Bainbridge found that people normally come to Christ and the church through the influence of relatives or close friends.[8]

Another study, concerning causes of growth and decline, found that the *attitude* of the members toward the worship and program of the church is the most important internal reason for growth. "Churches that grow are those able to generate high levels of membership satisfaction."[9] As members talk about the ways they are served by the congregation, the potential converts who trust them are attracted and the church grows.

c. Felt Needs

For some near neighbors an important area of need will be to find a place to serve. The congregation that provides them a job to do will improve its usefulness to them. They also need a place to be nurtured in the Bible. Prematurely giving these people classes to teach would be counterproductive. Training is needed.

When the Gallup Organization conducted its study of "The Unchurched American" in 1978, 52 percent who admitted being *more* active in church in the past said that they could "see themselves becoming a fairly active member of a church again." When these same people were asked what circumstances would result in their becoming active once more, the most frequent reply was: "If I could find a pastor or church friends with whom I could openly discuss my religious doubts." The second highest response indicated a similar need, namely: "If I found a pastor or church friends with whom I could openly discuss my spiritual needs." Small congregations that are willing to pay the necessary price for becoming more useful in meeting these kinds of needs can expect to grow.[10]

Small congregations cannot meet all needs. However, as the members work together, their usefulness and effectiveness can be broadened.

Individual small churches that desire growth pay the price of analyzing what *they* do best and what their *near* neighbors need most. It is when they identify their strengths and mesh *these* strengths with the needs of potential converts that substantive growth occurs.

Summary

Every small church must courageously face earnest self-analysis. At the same time they must believe that most small congregations *can* grow if they want to grow—and are willing to pay the necessary price.

The first question churches should prayerfully ask of themselves is *Does our congregation, both pastor and people, really want to grow?* Some will grow by planting new congregations. Others will create vital small groups as they grow.

The cost of church growth for small congregations sometimes comes high. The price to be paid will vary with different church situations. However, there are three general areas of cost in which most congregations will need to pay some price. These may be put in question form:

1. *Will our congregation pay the price to remove unnecessary social barriers between us and people in spiritual need?*

2. *Will our congregation pay the price of making the church physically more accessible to the groups for whom God has given us special responsibility?*

3. *Will our congregation pay the price of meeting the specific needs of our near neighbors?*

This spiritual exercise in self-analysis is costly in itself. It demands honesty and objectivity, but growth is far more likely to occur if these issues are faced.

The analysis of these barriers to growth and the subsequent organization for change may best be accomplished in consultation with those trained in church growth analysis. Small churches tend to be reluctant to seek such assistance because of the cost or because of their accustomed informal family style of decision-making. However, for those congregations interested in changing their growth patterns and who have been unable to bring about that change on their own, the services of interested, qualified outsiders can be an extremely worthwhile investment. And church growth is, indeed, worth any investment that is required.

DISCUSSION QUESTIONS

1. Does your church really want to grow? What are the advantages and disadvantages of growth in your situation?
2. Who are the specific groups of people for whom God has given you special responsibility?
3. How can you get closer to people in these groups? What unnecessary barriers are there between you and them?
4. How accessible are your facilities to the people you need to reach?
5. What needs do your near neighbors have that you can meet? How useful is the program of your church from their point of view?
6. What honest analysis concerning the growth potential of your church is being done? What more could be done?

A Family in Mission

by Rev. Ron Benefiel

If Janet and I had really known what we were getting ourselves into, we might not have accepted the assignment. But since the district superintendent asked us to go, and since he said there was no one else available that he could appoint, we went. It was just a little farming community out in the middle of the California desert. Not many people live there, and there are few Nazarenes—10 members—6 of them active. I could tell from the start that it was going to be a whole new experience in working with a "small congregation."

Janet, my wife, and I soon discovered that the 25 to 30 people who usually attended had high expectations of the pastor and wife. Just about whatever needed to be done, we did. I set out an hour early each Sunday picking up kids for Sunday School. Janet taught the class for children and I

REV. RON BENEFIEL,
doctoral candidate at the University of Southern California, pastors First Church of the Nazarene in Los Angeles. He has taught at Azusa Pacific University, Azusa, Calif., and has served as associate pastor in several Churches of the Nazarene. Rev. Benefiel is founder of P. F. Bresee Institute, for urban ministry training, and is a member of the steering committee of the Association of Nazarene Sociologists of Religion.

taught the adults. When the worship service began, Janet led the singing and I played the piano. One Sunday I prayed before the offering and then came down from the platform and collected the offering! Before the message, Janet would take the children out for junior church and I would preach to "the remnant." After the benediction we'd pile all the kids into the car and take them home. Mission accomplished.

We profited greatly from the experience out in the desert with that small congregation. Even though the work was demanding and the visible rewards few, we became acquainted with a group of people who had survived as a small congregation for over 20 years. There was something there that seemed to persist, something worth maintaining and protecting. There was something in the relationships of the people that was timeless and solid . . . and valuable.

As I have reflected on those memorable days, along with some years of experiences in other small congregations, I have come to believe that the unique quality of the small congregation is the ability to function as a family.

Brothers, Sisters, and Third Cousins

The similarities between a small congregation and a family are so striking that the comparison is too much to resist. For one thing, when all the interrelationships are considered, many small congregations are literally composed of two or three family networks and a few "adopted" family members. More than one prospective pastor, while interviewing with the church board, has been surprised by the discovery that the board consisted of seven people named "Jones" and their three cousins.

But even beyond the sense in which small congregations are literal family groups, there are a number of ways in which small congregations seem to function like a family. Let's consider three of them.

1. *Intimacy*

Intimacy was the underlying theme of the small congregation my dad pastored while I was growing up. Everybody knew everybody else and knew them well. If one of our "church family" was absent, we were aware of it and usually knew why. If some new family happened to be present, their unfamiliar faces immediately identified them as visitors. We worked, played, ate, sang, and worshiped together as a unit—a family. The intimacy was not just in the "knowing" of each other, it was also in the "being known." There seemed to be a feeling of "being at home with each other" among those who were on the inside. As in a family, we experienced love, care, and emotional support—intimacy.

Intimacy is undoubtedly one of the greatest strengths of the small congregation. *It is little wonder that so many people find satisfaction in small congregations where they feel such close communion.* However, this may also represent a problem. Assuming that part of the church's goal is to minister effectively to its community, the high priority placed on intimacy within the congregation may sometimes be a hindrance in achieving that goal. Members of the congregation may fear that if the congregation begins to grow, it might become impossible for them to know everyone as they once did. They may be afraid that the closeness they value so greatly will be diluted or destroyed. Like a family that values times of being alone together, they may resist the incorporation of newcomers for the sake of safeguarding a sense of intimacy.

2. *Heritage*

Religion, in almost any form at nearly any time in history, has had the remarkable capability of transmitting cultural values from one generation to the next. The modern-day small congregation is a prime example.

Carl Dudley has pointed out that larger churches tend to focus on the future while the smaller churches tend to focus on the past.[1] The small congregation's ability to pass on cultural values may be considered one of its greatest strengths, but it can be one of its weaknesses. *It is a strength in that it provides for the members of the small congregation a certain continuity with the past; an identity that has accumulated meaning over a number of years.* In answer to the question, "Who am I?" the member of the small congregation can proudly say: "I am an Elm Street Methodist" much in the same way that he or she might sense a certain identity by belonging to a particular family. In the small congregation there is a kind of belonging, an identity that seems secure and permanent. It emerges from the past and promises to remain steady in the future.

However, the small congregation's commitment to preserve its heritage may also have its dangers. With its focus on the past, it is typically conservative, clinging tenaciously to the familiar and often resisting innovation. This tendency to resist change may limit the congregation's ability to effectively relate the gospel to the outside world—a society undergoing "future shock."

The Jews of Jesus' day did a great job of preserving the values and customs for their own benefit and for that of future generations. However, it might be argued that they failed in their calling to take the message into a world that needed to hear it. Completely ingrown, they failed to minister to those beyond their own walls.

The small congregation in today's society may be subject to the same potential weakness. For if the church's resistance to change insulates it from a changing world, how can it minister effectively to that world?

3. *Boundaries*

Sociologist David Kanter, an expert in family relations,

has pointed out the necessary role that boundaries play in the health and well-being of the family.

Family boundaries are the rules, traditions, and attitudes that separate a family, to some degree, from the rest of the world.[2] At one extreme, if family boundaries are wide *open*, there is little distinction between that family and the outside world. The border lines are "fuzzy." Such a family loses much of its ability to protect its members from unwanted outside influences. There is characteristically little discipline, little sense of family identity and little meaning in belonging to the family. Members are left without the awareness of security or safety that families usually provide. Boundaries between the family and the outside world are essential to its survival.

Alternatively, family boundaries may also be quite *closed*. They may be so restrictive that family members are not just protected, they are denied contact with many or most individuals outside the family. A closed family may result when, in the face of a menacing society, the family reacts by trying to isolate itself from the threats of the outside world. As a result, the boundaries between the family and the rest of the world may become rigid, inflexible, and nearly impenetrable.

Churches also have boundaries that protect and distance members from the outside world. As in the family, these boundaries are necessary if the congregation is going to exist at all. Without sufficient boundaries the congregation would have little cohesiveness or uniqueness. It would be like a raindrop that happened to fall into a lake. It would be totally engulfed in the larger social context.

The church needs boundaries that furnish those on the inside a sense of being separate and unique. Boundaries can provide a feeling of safety and security to church members, protecting them from a hostile world with all of its enticements to sin. The church needs rules and guidelines and disciplines not only for moral and ethical reasons but also for group identity and morale.

In the face of a threatening world, agreed-upon values and disciplines can become the focus of a common commitment—rallying the congregation around meaningful issues. Boundaries between the church and the world also alert those outside to the fact that the church is different—that it provides some kind of alternative to the commonly accepted secular life-style. The church needs boundaries that set it apart from the secular world.

The tendency for small congregations, however, is to develop boundaries that are so closed they are difficult to penetrate. The congregation, of course, in maintaining closed boundaries may be trying to protect what it considers to be of utmost importance. It may be trying to sustain a righteous community of believers in an unrighteous world, a loving "family" in a hostile world.

But there is a real disadvantage for the church that chooses to keep its boundaries securely closed—nobody can get in from the outside. The church's mission to effectively minister to the community may be severely limited. In protecting itself from the outside world, the small congregation may also be distancing itself from people in the community who desperately need the benefit of the ministry of the church in their lives.

The image is that of a fully equipped hospital with a well-trained staff that refuses to admit patients. The reason being that as patients are admitted and treated, the equipment might get broken or the staff might catch some unwanted disease. Or, worse yet, the patients might interfere with the unity and solidarity of the staff.

It is not so much that the small congregation tends to be unfriendly. To the contrary. It may be very friendly, just as family members would be toward a guest in their home. However, also like a family, it may be very difficult and require much time for the guest to be accepted as an insider—as "one of the family." In between the time that visitors are welcomed and the time they are fully accepted as family members (if they stick around that long), they may feel excluded and left out. They may feel awkward, as though they are attending a party without an invitation.

Willimon and Wilson put it this way, "One reason newcomers to the small church sometimes receive the impression that the church is closed, cold, exclusive, and reluctant to open itself up to new members, is that the small church behaves as a family does."[3] And like a family, the small congregation may be hesitant, or even unwilling, to fully accept new members into the fellowship. Boundaries are necessary, but closed boundaries may become a liability.

The Call Beyond the Threshold

As a church, part of the calling of the small congregation is undoubtedly to function like a family (Gal. 6:10; 1 Cor. 12). The small congregation generally fulfills this part of its calling well. Nowhere are the titles "brother" and "sister" more appropriate than in the family and in the small congregation. But to be a family is not the total calling of the small congregation. The first priority of the church is always to mission. It is called to be "the salt of the earth" (Matt. 5:13). It is not to hide its light, but to be "the light of the world" (Matt. 5:14). It is called to "go and make disciples" (Matt. 28:19-20). It is called to feed the hungry, clothe the naked, and visit those who are sick or in prison (Matt. 25:31-46). Certainly the small congregation as part of the Church of Jesus Christ is called to MISSION.

This may pose a real problem for the typical small congregation. For here we evidence *conflicting demands* pulling it in two different directions. *The demand to be the family of God and the demand to do the work of God. Intimacy versus out-*

reach—maintenance versus mission. For some small congregations this is no problem at all. Many smaller churches are
actively involved in reaching out to their community. For
many, growth has added an exciting dimension to their fellowship. But for too many small congregations growth is neg-
ligible or nonexistent. They seem to have grown accustomed
to a very typical mold—a sort of comfortable rut.

At one time or another, you may have heard the frus-
trated pastor of a small congregation complain, "They just
don't want to grow!" But most of the members of small congregations would disagree. They really would like their
church to grow. They very much would like to be fulfilling
their calling as a church—to minister to the community.

If there is resistance to mission and growth in the small
congregation, it may not be so much that the members do not
want the church to grow; it may be that the *cost* of growth
seems to be too great. Subconsciously, members may sense
that to grow may mean that the intimacy, the security, the
traditional methods that are so familiar and so valuable may
be threatened. This represents a cost they may be unwilling
to consider.

How can the apparent conflict be resolved? In the small
congregation, how can the sense of family be protected while
the mission of the church is being fulfilled? On the one hand,
this may appear to be an unsolvable dilemma. In some situations the church membership may seem to be so committed
to "closed boundaries" that any effort to move them appears
futile. But on the other hand, with a generous dose of "tender
loving care" and with a sensitivity to the leading of the Holy
Spirit, pastors and laymen working together may be able to
see some of the closed boundaries begin to open. I am not
suggesting that churches reconsider their commitment to
moral and ethical standards. I am not suggesting that they
relinquish their commitment to being a family. Quite to the

contrary. Small congregations *can* take seriously the call to mission. They can have the best of both worlds.

With this in mind, I offer the following suggestions to pastors and laymen of small congregations interested in seeing their church respond to the call.

1. *Appreciate the Strengths*

The small congregation has many valuable qualities that are worth protecting. It often provides a deep sense of meaning and identity for its members. There is something very beautiful and precious about the relationship bonds. Members are typically going to protect the values, traditions, and relationships that mean so much to them. This is the strength of the small congregation. *Learn to appreciate the familylike qualities of the small congregation and recognize them as assets.*

2. *Earn the Right to Lead*

More than one pastor has made the mistake of thinking that with the title of "pastor" comes the authority and privilege of leadership. Formally this may be true. However, in most congregations there is an informal leadership base that has developed over a period of years and has survived several pastoral changes. In most instances, it will be counterproductive to try to compete with those who are the informally recognized leaders of the congregation.

Learn to work closely with the leaders of the congregation. They are not the enemy. They almost always want the church to succeed. Many times they have already given much of their life to the church. They have the potential of being the greatest supporters of its ongoing ministry.

Develop a trust relationship with those who hold informal power in the congregation. *Become a part of "the family."* It may take some time for them to see that you value the qualities and strengths of the familylike relationships in the church and that you have no intention of destroying those qualities. You may be entering as an outsider whom they have invited into their family. Join them. Become part of the family. Earn the right to lead.

3. *Lead On*

Having earned the privilege, take the lead in reaching out into the community. Generally, members of a small congregation are quite aware that, as a church, they need to be ministering to their community. They love their church and have a deep pride in it. If their church begins to minister effectively in the community, it could bring them a great sense of achievement and satisfaction. It could make them proud to be part of a church that is trying to accomplish what they agree is the mission of the church. However, to reach out beyond themselves will usually mean that some things will have to change. And change can be very threatening.

Begin by exploring avenues of ministry that are relatively nonthreatening to the nature of the fellowship. Work *with* those in your church, not *around* them.

As you encounter resistance to the changes, be sensitive to the feelings of those who are hesitant. You may be treading on "sacred ground." The congregation's resistance to change may be a valuable warning to you. It may tell you where you need to go slow. Often there is a very good historical reason for the resistance. Be sensitive to the feelings of those who are hesitant. Include them in the process of discovering the mission of the church. Ask them what kind of mission they think the church should be involved in. Lead them in accomplishing their new goals.

Finally, set the example. Merely telling others that the church needs to reach out to the community may bring verbal agreement but little action. Show them what it means to reach out by your own example. Invite key leaders to go calling with you in the community. Invite them to help lead a neighborhood Bible study in a member's home. Help them discover the dimensions of meaning and satisfaction that involvement in the mission of the church can bring to the "family" they love so much.

One Church's Attempt

My wife and I were once a part of a small church located in a community that was undergoing significant ethnic and socioeconomic changes. The congregation enjoyed a 25-year history out of which a beautiful, solid sense of family had developed. The pastor was committed to his people and had a vision for ministry in the community.

But the more the community changed, the more difficult it became for the church to reach out into the neighborhood and the easier it was for the members to settle for a ministry to the church "family." But the pastor persisted in keeping the vision of ministry to the community before the people, and after considerable deliberation, they took a risky step forward. A Spanish-speaking ministry was commissioned. This was difficult for many of the people. It meant some things were changing. It created some insecurity about the use of their building.

In the course of events there was a pastoral change and the new pastor picked up where the previous pastor left off. The people began to catch the vision. They began to accompany the pastor in an effort to reach out into the community. In less than a year, the English-speaking congregation has now grown from an average of 35 to an average of over 90 in morning worship. They have recently organized a Chinese ministry in addition to the Spanish-speaking ministry. The people have caught the vision of the mission.

This is not to say that this activity has solved all the problems of this small congregation; in some ways they have added to them. But the rewards of ministering to the community, of starting to break down some closed boundaries, have so far been more than worth the risk. The church is beginning to fulfill its calling in a new and vital way.

Call to Mission

The small congregation is alive and thriving in our society. It has not only survived but often has been an important stabilizing force in an unstable society.

The great strength of the small congregation is its ability to function like a family. It has provided love, warmth, security, and intimacy for its members while protecting them from the menacing dangers of the outside world.

If there has been a weakness that has frequently developed in the small congregation, it has been its unwillingness or inability to involve itself fully in the mission of the church by ministering effectively to the surrounding community.

A church that committed itself to mission but had no sense of family would be missing a significant part of its calling—the unity and brotherhood of the saints. But by the same token, a church that enjoyed the intimacy of familylike relationships but failed in its calling to minister to those outside the church would also be falling far short of its potential.

The challenge before the small congregation is *not* to forsake its heritage or its unique sense of togetherness and common identity. These and other values are all too rare in our society as it is. But the challenge is to accept the call to mission even if it means some changes need to take place. It does not need to be a question of either family or mission. The challenge for the small congregation is to be "a family in mission."

DISCUSSION QUESTIONS

1. How is your church like a family? What illustrations of mutual support and intimacy in your church come to mind?
2. Would you say that the boundaries to your church fellowship are relatively open or largely closed? To substantiate your conclusion, reflect on how many people from the community have been *fully* accepted into the fellowship in the last year. 2 years? 5 years?
3. How is your community changing? What kinds of ministries are needed in your community?
4. How is your church currently ministering to your community? How much of the ministry of your church involves your members actually going out into the community?
5. How is your church planning to minister to your community in the coming years? When you look at the church calendar, what events or emphases are scheduled that will help your church reach out into your community?

11

Being a Real Church

by Rev. Bill M. Sullivan

The small church is a *real* church; it is a family in mission and a colony of God's kingdom on earth. It is authentic to its members and useful to God. But its limited size may lead to poor self-image and identity problems.

The writers of this book have presented the small congregations as a justifiable expression of the Church of Jesus Christ and as full partners in the mission of our Lord. So the pastor and people of a small congregation need not feel unimportant or insignificant. They are, in fact, a vital part of the Kingdom.

If you are one of the "under 100 members" congregations that predominate in the Christian church today, you have sufficient reason for positive attitudes about your church and its place in the Kingdom.

As you view your church in this light I would like to

REV. BILL M. SULLIVAN
is the director of the Division of Church Growth and Evangelism Ministries for the Church of the Nazarene. Prior to coming to the denomination's International Headquarters in Kansas City, he served as district superintendent in North Carolina and as a pastor in Colorado. Rev. Sullivan is in a doctoral program at Fuller Theological Seminary, Pasadena, Calif.

suggest three commitments that I believe will keep a small church vital and victorious.

Be Realistic

The colossus complex has infected our culture for many years; it may remain for a long time into the future. You can't change that and don't be surprised when church leaders reflect a "bigger-is-better" mentality. We are all affected by this cultural characteristic to a greater degree than we would care to admit.

So accept the existence of the colossus concept, but don't allow it to intimidate you. Remember, size is relative. What would be considered a big church in a small town may be merely mediocre in a large city. At the same time, many churches have an influence out of proportion to their numerical size, such as the Church of the Savior in Washington, D.C., and the Salvation Army. Recall what theologian Kenneth Grider stated in chapter 3: "Scripture never states that any of the churches were either large or small . . . the size of the churches does not seem to be of great significance to the [Bible's] writers."

Keep in mind also that the small congregation is a fully authentic church. As Paul Bassett's lesson from history reveals, the nature of the church does not require a large number of members in order to be complete. Where two or three believers gather in the name of Jesus they are joined by the living presence of Christ, and you have an authentic Christian church that God wants to use in winning His world.

Keep your attention focused on *your significance.* The presence of so many small churches doesn't mean that small is ideal. Rather, service to out-of-the-way places and groups of people is the goal. Some of these groups will never be reached by large churches. So *your* church is significant.

Be realistic about the characteristics of your church. The

small congregation is not a miniature large church. Consequently, do not expect to operate like big organizations. As Ron Benefiel says, think more in terms of a family-type relationship. This may limit to some degree the spectrum of people you can effectively reach and help. On the other hand, such specialization will increase your ability to reach certain groups of needy people.

Also realize a key point made by Ken Crow, that geographical location affects the potential for growth. While an especially gifted leader may be able to "work miracles" anywhere, this is far from the norm. Members of the small church should make the most of the location that God has given them. The pastor must not lose heart in the midst of static or declining population. This is especially a danger if the community appears to be resistant.

Small churches located in changing communities present special challenges to both pastor and people. They need not only think through their situation carefully and pray for divine guidance but, if possible, also seek the advice of competent and caring consultants.

Conditions exist that, for the most part, are beyond our control, yet they have a profound effect on a church's ability to minister. Churches and their leaders should be realistic about these and other circumstances. But being realistic is *not* the same as being pessimistic. The small church has reason for hope.

Be Optimistic

Perhaps the clearest affirmation of this present volume is that the small church has strengths that, if not unique, are at least typical of small congregations. The paramount strength is *intimacy.* Charles Gailey is right in saying that many people want face-to-face interaction with people in a caring fellowship. The small congregation usually provides this without organizing for it. Encounter is inevitable in a group of 50 to 75 adults who meet at a common time and place on a regular basis.

Another strength of the small church is *participation*. It is generally agreed that a higher percentage of the members of a small organization participate in the activities of the group than in a large organization. Whether there is more opportunity for involvement in a small church than a large one may be debatable, but it is certain that there is plenty of opportunity for participation in the small congregation. And in the small church there is the added motivation of necessity.

A *favorable environment for leadership* development is another strength of the small church. The need for involvement calls forth potential leaders. On-the-job training, where high performance standards are not required and where feedback is immediate and encouragement is personal, contributes to the development of leaders.

When the members of a small church reflect on these strengths they will realize that there is substantial cause for optimism about the quality and attractiveness of their "little" church. Furthermore, they need not be discouraged over the weaknesses that are often enumerated. They can hope for genuine improvement when they work on these.

Some weaknesses are only strengths carried to the extreme. Exclusiveness is intimacy overextended. The problem can usually be overcome by education and planning. Exclusiveness is usually unintentional. When people discover how outsiders perceive them, they are generally eager to change their behavior. Planning programs to incorporate outsiders will frequently ease the problem.

Lack of organization and haphazard procedures are often the product of familiarity. In the family atmosphere "putting on airs" is out of place. But this sometimes results in appearing "hokey." Fortunately, this too can be readily overcome—and without conflict. Excellence in ministry need not threaten familiarity.

Other weaknesses that seem apparent may not be real. For example, the small church may look unsuccessful but may be involved in a very worthwhile ministry. It may be more evangelistically effective than churches several times its size.

Likewise, though resources appear to be limited in the small church, they are probably adequate. Ministry may not require nearly as much resource as we assume. The New Testament church had few material resources, but they accomplished their mission to an amazing degree. As someone has said, "The Early Church lacked everything we have and yet possessed exactly what we need."

Another reason for members of small congregations to be optimistic about their churches is that they have options. They are not hopelessly locked into the status quo. It is true that change does not come easily but it can be achieved.

Challenging a small church to become involved in a specialized ministry can be very successful if it doesn't contradict the culture, disrupt vital relationships, or financially overtax the church. Wise leadership, both pastoral and lay, can avoid such needless conflict.

An exciting option for a small church is to sponsor the establishment of a new congregation. Recent changes in church planting concepts make this mission enterprise much more feasible for a group with limited means. Such involvement will usually produce great satisfaction for the sponsoring church and, not infrequently, a new spurt of growth at home.

The potential for expansion and growth in the small church should not be discounted, however. Most churches probably can grow if, as Ken Crow reminds us, they really want to grow and are willing to pay the price. The small church *can* grow, in most instances *should* grow, and if properly directed *will* grow. It has demonstrated an ability to draw its present number of people together. It grew from zero to its present size. *Whatever it did to attract the original group it can, in all likelihood, do again.* If it did, it would grow.

It should be recognized that the small church has grown by merely maintaining its size. If a church organizes with 25 members and 10 years later still has the same number of people, it must have received new members to make up for the loss of those who moved away or died. While this has not expanded the church above its original size, it has at least not declined.

This is important because the small church is not only reasonably effective in growth, it is also quite susceptible to membership attrition. The small church is in a continual process of growth to compensate for its losses. This could prompt us to say that not only *has* the small church grown but it is also growing and does grow. So growth is an available option to the small church.

Not only does the small congregation have strengths and options, it also has resources. First of all, it has its own people plus the people in the community. People solve all problems—as well as create them! They give money, provide leadership, and dilute conflict. Reach people and resources will multiply. People are a much greater resource than money or facilities.

The people in the community should not be overlooked as a resource. Many of them are considerably more aware of our presence and concerned about our needs than we think. My first district superintendent, Dr. O. J. Finch, instructed me carefully that "people will help you do something, but they won't help you do nothing."

The pastor is also a distinct resource. His call to minister, commitment to obedience, and his training in the Word of God is a powerful plus. He should be prayed for, encouraged, and followed in pursuing the mission of the church.

Most of all, it should be remembered that God is as available to the small church as He is to any size church. With God all things are possible. The songwriter is right in declaring that "Little is much when God is in it."

So the small church has far greater resources than it has imagined. As Jack Nash declares, it can be optimistic because it has the resources to capitalize on its strengths and exercise its options. Such optimism leads to action—appropriate mission.

Be Evangelistic

Ignoring the colossus complex does not require rejecting evangelistic activity. *Seeking the salvation of the lost is not, as some may think, a disguised numerolatry. It is, indeed, involvement in the principal work of the church.*

God's grand plan is the redemption of His creation. This is to be understood in its ultimate sense. In the light of His redemptive purpose God is not unconcerned about the quality and conditions of life, but such temporal issues must not cloud eternal realities. The redemption of man from sin is primary.

It is sin that has produced estrangement and death. Sin has separated us from God. The heart of the problem of the world is sin.

The prioritization of evangelism does not deny the importance of compassionate ministries. To the contrary, it calls the church to see persons holistically and seek their liberation from sin and its consequences. And it charges the church to minister to the needy in Jesus' name. For He who saves is He who first "so loved the world."

However, within the reality of God's compassion is the inescapable necessity of salvation through faith in Jesus Christ. It is in this sense that Jesus declared He came to seek and to save the lost. His mission was to bring salvation to people. It is also the first order of the church's mission.

Mission is an assigned task. It is not merely the doing of something worthwhile. It is doing what Christ has charged us to do. Mission may include many activities but it is primarily rescue—saving the lost.

But this rescue effort is not to be thought of in narrow terms. Evangelism itself must be holistic. As Christians we are instructed to be salt and light. But evangelism is more than just being. Christ has charged us to go and tell the good news, but evangelism is more than informing people about the good news. Jesus declared that a new birth is necessary, yet evangelism is more than an experience. The Great Commission charges Christians with the responsibility of "teaching them," yet evangelism is more than indoctrination. Evangelism is, in fact, all of these and is not complete until it has resulted in obedience to Jesus Christ as Lord.

Just as evangelism is to be understood in broad terms, so mission comprehends a wide range of ministries. Such ministries are not sidelines. They are part of the mosaic of God's grand plan of redemption. The focus of the design is on personal salvation from sin, but the picture is incomplete without the whole mosaic.

So the final word to the church involved in mission is to seek the lost *as Christ sought them.* He went from town to town proclaiming the good news. He took with Him followers who would later extend His ministry. Wherever He went He was attentive to the physical and emotional needs of all classes of people. He had compassion for the masses. He healed the sick. He spoke out for justice. And He was especially accepting of the social outcast.

He took leadership of a small group to train them to carry on His redemptive mission. It was a fellowship, but it was a fellowship with a purpose—a family in mission.

Forgiveness of the sinner and restoration of the outcast

were trademarks of His ministry. He was and is the Savior. When we do His work in the world we are involved in rescue and restoration. "We are therefore Christ's ambassadors, as though God were making his appeal through us. We implore [the lost] on Christ's behalf: Be reconciled to God" (2 Cor. 5:20).

This appeal through us is powerful because of His presence in us. Evangelistic effort is motivated, enabled, and authenticated by the Holy Spirit. This is true for individual believers and for churches. It was the coming of the Holy Spirit on the Day of Pentecost that produced witness, conviction, and conversion. Without Him the Early Church could not have existed. He is no less important to the church today.

The evangelistic effectiveness of the smaller church depends on the Holy Spirit. Methods are necessary but not sufficient. Churches of all sizes have experienced the frustration of striving to do a great work for God without God. But in the power of the Holy Spirit thousands of small churches have experienced the joy of reaching people in their community and witnessing the miracle of spiritual transformation.

That joy awaits any church that seeks to fulfill its responsibility in the power of the Holy Spirit. When the Holy Spirit is the resource, any disadvantage of the smaller church isn't particularly important. He can bring victory to any circumstance.

The greatest discovery a smaller church can make is not some organizational strategy or programmatic method but the spiritual power of the Holy Spirit. This is not an oversimplification. The church that seeks the Holy Spirit, waits for His coming, commits its resources to His use and follows His directions will experience one spiritual miracle after another.

So do not let the failure of human methods discourage and defeat you. With new hope and courage allow the power of the Holy Spirit to become a mighty dynamic in your church. Then the smaller churches of the land will bring revival and evangelism to masses of people, and the era of the smaller church will have come.

Reference Notes

Chapter 1:

1. *The Height of Your Life* (Boston: Little, Brown and Company, 1980).

2. Quoted in Bob Benson, *In Quest of the Shared Life* (Nashville: Impact Books, 1981), 124.

3. Edward C. Stewart, *American Cultural Patterns: A Cross-Cultural Perspective* (LaGrange Park, Ill.: Intercultural Network, 1972), 68. (Paraphrased in C. Peter Wagner, *Church Growth and the Whole Gospel: A Biblical Mandate* [San Francisco: Harper and Row, Publishers, 1981], 63.)

4. (Kansas City: Beacon Hill Press of Kansas City, 1982), 8.

5. Reuben Welch discusses this point at length in his book titled *We Really Do Need Each Other* (Nashville: Impact, n.d.).

6. Lyle E. Schaller, *The Small Church Is Different!* (Nashville: Abingdon, 1982), 144.

7. Reference to article by Donald Golliher, "Evangelical Benefits," *Herald of Holiness*, Aug. 1, 1982, p. 11.

8. (Nashville: Abingdon, 1978), front cover and p. 176.

9. *The Small Church: Valid, Vital, Victorious* (Valley Forge, Pa.: Judson Press, 1975), 110.

10. *Koinonia* is the Greek New Testament word for "fellowship of believers." It implies, both, *being* together and *doing* (i.e., Kingdom-building) together.

Chapter 2:

1. Jackson W. Carroll, *Small Churches Are Beautiful* (San Francisco: Harper & Row, 1977). Cf. also Dudley, *Making the Small Church Effective;* William H. Willimon and Robert L. Wilson, *Preaching and Worship in the Small Church* (Nashville: Abingdon, 1980); Maner, *Making the Small Church Grow;* and Schaller, *The Small Church Is Different.*

2. Willimon and Wilson, *Preaching and Worship* (Nashville: Abingdon, 1980), 20.

3. Neil J. Smelser, *Sociology* (Englewood Cliffs, N.J.: Prentice-Hall, 1981), 30.

4. Cf. Ferdinand Töennies, *Community and Society* (New York: Harper & Row, 1957).

5. David O. Moberg, *The Church as a Social Institution* (Englewood Cliffs, N.J.: Prentice-Hall, 1962), 417.

6. I am referring here to *active* participation.

7. Wayne Oates, *The Christian Pastor* (Philadelphia: Westminster, 1982), 156.

8. Arthur C. Tennies, "The Social and Theological Images of the Small Church," in Carroll, ed.: *Small Churches Are Beautiful,* 65.

9. Schaller, *Small Church Is Different,* 33.

10. Tennies in *Small Churches Are Beautiful,* 64.

11. Michael O. Christensen, "We Can Be Small Without Being Little About It," *Grassroots,* vol. 4, nos. 2 and 3 (Winter and Spring 1981), 25.

Chapter 5:

1. There are a number of sources from which such information can be gathered. A nearby college should have local economic, social, family, political, and religious data available. Service clubs have networks of associations from which information can be gathered. The Junior Chamber of Commerce is a fruitful source of community happenings. The local ministerial association can supply information concerning the area.

2. This problem was recognized by Samuel Blizzard in 1956—see Samuel Blizzard, "The Minister's Dilemma," *Christian Century,* vol. 73 (1956): 508-9. Blizzard identified six different parts of the minister's role: preacher, pastor, priest, teacher, organizer, and administrator. He pointed out the problem that the minister must spend most of his time in administration and organization, the two areas in which he probably has the least amount of expertise.

Chapter 6:

1. (Kansas City: Beacon Hill Press of Kansas City, 1981), 21.

2. Ibid., 109.

3. Ibid., 9.

Chapter 7:

1. Dr. Bresee went so far as to declare that everyone in the world should have the opportunity to hear the gospel once before any one person hears it twice.

2. Lyle E. Schaller, ed., *Creative Leadership Series: Assimilating New Members* (Nashville: Parthenon Press, 1978), 58 ff.

3. The office of "general superintendent" is the highest elected position within the Church of the Nazarene. Throughout the years, the total number of general superintendents has varied. Presently, there are six.

The "General Assembly" is normally held every four years, and is the highest legislative body within the church. Delegates are elected from all of the districts. Official policies are enacted.

4. This quotation is taken from the official Minutes of the 1948 General Assembly. Technically, such statements do not constitute official policy, but when spoken by a general superintendent they have great authority and influence.

5. These statistics were compiled by the office of the general secretary of the Church of the Nazarene.

Chapter 8:

1. *When in Doubt Hug 'Em!* (Atlanta: John Knox Press, 1978), 13.

2. John Wimber's lecture given to ministers of the North Carolina District of the Church of the Nazarene.

3. "The Temptation of Ministry: Improving Your Reserve" —an interview with Charles Swindoll by the editor of *Leadership Magazine, Christianity Today,* vol. 3, no. 4 (Fall, 1982):19.

4. *Small Church Is Different,* 9, 58.

5. (Nashville: Abingdom, 1972), 107.

Chapter 9:

1. C. Peter Wagner, *Your Church Can Grow* (Glendale, Calif.: Regal Books, 1976), 49.

2. Robert Currie, Alan Gilbert, and Lee Horsley, *Churches and Churchgoers* (Oxford: Clarendon Press, 1977), 7. This is a study that focuses on nearly 300 years of church growth and decline in England.

3. Carl S. Dudney, "The Small Church as Primary Group," in *Catalyst* (Waco, Tex.: Word, 1979), vol. 11, no. 12:4-6.

4. H. H. Gerth and C. Wright Mills, *From Max Weber* (New York: Oxford University Press, 1946), 316; Ernst Troeltsch, *The So-*

cial Teaching of the Christian Churches, trans. by Olive Wynon (New York: Macmillan, 1931), 331; Kurt H. Wolff, *The Sociology of Georg Simmel* (New York: The Free Press, 1950), 87-90.

5. Mendell Taylor, *Handbook of Historical Documents of the Church of the Nazarene* (Unpublished), 183.

6. Timothy Smith, *Called unto Holiness* (Kansas City: Nazarene Publishing House, 1962), 113-14.

7. William M. Newman and Peter L. Halverson, *Patterns in Pluralism: A Portrait of American Religion* (Washington, D.C.: Glenmary Research Center, 1980), 52.

8. Rodney Stark and William Sims Bainbridge, "Networks of Faith: Interpersonal Bonds and Recruitment to Cults and Sects" (*American Journal of Sociology,* 1980, 85), 1376-95.

9. Wade Clark Roof, Dean R. Hoge, John E. Dyble, and C. Kirk Hadaway, "Factors Producing Growth or Decline in United Presbyterian Congregations," in *Understanding Church Growth and Decline,* Dean R. Hoge and David A. Roozen, eds. (New York: The Pilgrim House, 1979), 212.

10. The Gallup Organization, The Unchurched American Study.

Chapter 10:

1. *Unique Dynamics of the Small Church* (Washington, D.C.: The Alban Institute, Inc., 1977), 10.

2. David Kanter, *Inside the Family* (San Francisco: Josey-Bass Publishers, 1975).

3. William H. Willimon and Robert L. Wilson, *Preaching and Worship in the Small Church,* Creative Leadership Series. Lyle E. Schaller, ed. (Nashville: Abingdon, 1980), 66.

Bibliography

Blizzard, Samuel. "The Minister's Dilemma." *Christian Century*, vol. 73 (1956).

Carroll, Jackson W. (3rd). *Small Churches Are Beautiful.* San Francisco: Harper and Row, 1977.

Currie, Robert; Gilbert, Alan; and Horsley, Lee. *Churches and Churchgoers.* Oxford: Clarendon Press, 1977.

Dudley, Carl S. *Making the Small Church Effective.* Nashville: Abingdon, 1978.

———. *Unique Dynamics of the Small Church.* Washington, D.C.: The Alban Institute, Inc., 1977.

Hoge, Dean R.; and Roozen, David A. *Understanding Church Growth and Decline.* New York: The Pilgrim Press, 1979.

Kanter, David. *Inside the Family.* San Francisco: Josey-Bass Publishers, 1975.

Madsen, Paul O. *The Small Church: Valid, Vital, Victorious.* Valley Forge, Pa.: Judson Press, 1975.

Maner, Robert E. *Making the Small Church Grow.* Kansas City: Beacon Hill Press of Kansas City, 1982.

Mavis, W. Curry. *Advancing the Smaller Church.* Grand Rapids: Baker Book House, 1968.

McGavran, Donald. *Understanding Church Growth.* Grand Rapids: William B. Eerdmans Publishing Co., 1970.

Ray, David R. *Small Churches Are the Right Size.* New York: Pilgrim Press, 1982.

Schaller, Lyle. *The Small Church Is Different.* Nashville: Abingdon, 1982.

Simmel, Georg. "The Web of Group Affiliations" in *The Sociology of Georg Simmel* (Trans. by Kurt H. Wolff). New York: The Free Press, 1950.

Wagner, C. Peter. *Your Church Can Grow.* Glendale, Calif.: Regal Books, 1976.

Willimon, William H.; and Wilson, Robert L. *Preaching and Worship in the Small Church.* Creative Leadership Series. Lyle E. Schaller, ed. Nashville: Abingdon, 1980.

Index

151